Holiness Readings

A Selection of Papers on the
Doctrine, Experience, and Practice of Holiness

Reprinted from
The "War Cry"

Schmul Publishing Company
Nicholasville, Kentucky

Published by Schmul Publishing Co.
PO Box 776
Nicholasville, KY USA

Printed in the United States of America

ISBN 10: 0-88019-045-0
ISBN 13: 978-0-88019-045-9

CONTENTS.

PREFACE.

EVEN amongst our worst enemies it has been admitted that the strength of the Salvation Army lay in its Holiness teaching. Many indeed, have strangely represented that we teach nothing at all, but rely for success upon a mixture of gymnastics, music, and excitement. Hence they are still capable, after eighteen years of victory, of imagining that the army will some day suddenly collapse.

On the other hand there are those who solemnly shake their heads and declare that we teach a great deal too much, that we presume to hold up a standard to which no human being can ever attain, and of encouraging professions which can only be based on self-deception.

This book, as anyone may see at a glance, is not designed for contentious persons, but for those who want to be holy. We leave to schools of learning all discussions as to creeds and forms of speech. *We have to do with the streets;* and our one business is to direct into the way of peace those who want to find it.

Yes. The way of peace! although all our business is war. The Salvation Army must cease to exist whenever it loses the spirit of resolution to obey God, and cause him to be obeyed by all, which has always been its strength.

God asks and wishes to be obeyed. It is impossible that He should live on terms of intimate friendship with any of His subjects who are unwilling always to obey Him.

Most of God's professed servants say, I am willing to obey; but I cannot by reason of a division in my very nature which has been with me from my birth, which I cannot help, and which will be with me till I die.

To all such persons, who are nevertheless really wishful to escape from so miserable a state of things, may this book be indeed a messenger of peace.

To all those whom it may reach who have been content thus to excuse a life of mixed obedience and neglect, may this book be indeed a message of war. We say that God wishes to be obeyed, and if this be true, it is impossible to imagine Him unwilling to help us in every way that may be necessary to make this obedience possible.

Do you say, "I don't see it; I am puzzled about this; I have heard so many things on this subject that I really don't know what to believe." Can it be possible that God, who wishes you to obey Him, is not ready this moment to give you the very light you need to escape out of any bondage you may be suffering from into the liberty—the perfect liberty—from sin which you desire. Ask Him that, while you read these pages, they may help you to see your true position, and to find a way out of it into the right one.

Do you join in the common cry "about your circumstances"? Has it ever occurred to you that Enoch, a man who walked with God for 300 years, was not as you may have fancied, a prophet, living away from the rest of his race, but a married man, mingling all the time with the affairs of every-day life like other people, and surrounded like yourself with the ungodly world? Ask God to show you while you read these papers, written all of them by busy people, how to climb above your circumstances and walk with Him, even as Enoch did.

Is it some special weight, some old besetment, that appears to defy all your efforts to live a holy life, and before which you have become accustomed to give way with your helpless "I can't, I can't?" Then ask God to carry home to your heart, as you read, the echo of the cheery tramp of comrades who have learnt with a whole heart to follow Him who is always saying, "Fear not; for I have overcome the world."

God wishes to be obeyed. Not to have the unwilling service dragged out of a being, continually in division—continually discussing whether to obey or not; but with the glad eagerness of a child whose whole life is made radiant with the very thought of perfectly pleasing a loving parent.

The people who write these papers know the joy of this perfect *child life*. They know—they cannot express it to you—they just hold out a hand to help you up to it.

But, ah! I know what will prevent anyone from getting a blessing from the reading of this book. It is the unwillingness to leave ALL—to sacrifice ALL—to endure ALL. Do not hope to get any good out of this or any other book until you have come to that point to which, alas! so few come before they reach their deathbed—that point of willingness to leave all and follow Him who left all to seek for you, and to set you entirely free from sin, and fear, and spiritual weakness, that you might be a worthy labourer together with Him—a willing sharer of His sufferings, and so made fit to be a joint heir of His Crown.

OCTOBER, 1883.

READINGS ON HOLINESS.

The War Cry, No. 3.—JAN. 10, 1880.

A HIGHER UP RELIGION.

BY THE GENERAL.

I.

A LADY in one of our large cities, who takes a great interest in the doctrine of holiness, and who had sought me out because she had heard I loved the same blessed truth, gave me a rather curious account of the way in which the Lord had led her into the possession of this pearl of greatest price. She said, "I was a member of a Presbyterian Church, and had been converted for some years, but for a long time had been living in a poor half-hearted condition, my special difficulty being a hot and ready temper. I became convinced, and hardly knew how, that there must be a religious experience far beyond mine, but knew nothing about it. I talked to the Elders of my church, and sought counsel and guidance from my Minister, but they could tell me of nothing better. I prayed and searched my Bible, but got little forwarder, saving getting more deeply convicted that God had more of power and peace and joy for me than I had ever enjoyed. One day while walking in the city I saw on the other side the way a lady whom I knew by report to be more than ordinarily zealous in religion, and it occurred to me that she might be able to answer the problem that was perplexing and agitating my heart. At once I crossed the street, and, stopping her, said, 'Miss ——, can you tell me anything about "*a higher up religion?*"' I knew no manner by which to describe the experience that the Holy Ghost had set me hungering after, and so in the first words that came to my lips, that seemed best to indicate what I wanted, I called it 'a higher up religion.' She smiled, and said she did not exactly know what I meant, but some friend had lent her a book entitled 'Holiness by Faith.' She did not know what it contained, for she had shown it to her Minister, and he had pronounced it a very dangerous book, and charged her not to read a word in it, but to return it at once to the owner. I said, 'holiness,' that is what I want, and I suppose it must be had by faith. So I borrowed the book, read it, received the truth it taught, and more than this, according to its teachings I knelt down and trusted Jesus Christ to save me from my evil heart and from my bad temper, and he saved me there and then, and though many months have passed away He saves me to-day."

Now it seems to me that there are a good many people who have some inkling, some very strong suspicion that there must be a religion higher up than that which they enjoy; that for them there must be some joy and assurance and power in religion that is far above and beyond anything they experience and know. Something nearer in work and victory and glory to the plan and pattern and practice of the Prophets and Apostles and Martyrs; nearer the plan and pattern and practice of Jesus Christ, who is not only our Great Teacher and Redeemer, but our Example—something nearer the all-perfect principles and practice of the Great God Himself.

For my part, I hardly see how the religion of many of the professed followers of Jesus Christ could very well be *much lower down,* for is it not down, down, until nearly into the world itself, and lost sight of there. It dresses, and dances, and goes to theatres and concerts. It grubs after money, and idolizes, and todies and fawns on rank and position whatever the morals and godlessness of the said rank and station may be.

Low enough. It is consequently all uncertainty and weakness. Sure of nothing. It doubts the forgiveness of sins, doubts inspiration and hell, Calvary and immortality, and angels and devils, and God Himself so far as any active interference with the things of this present every day world is concerned; in short, all else that it cannot see and hear and in general apprehend and handle with its five bodily senses.

And what follows? Why the religion of to-day, this fashionable religion, even the very choicest of it sins and repents, and then sins again; the things that it would do those it does not, and the things that it would not do those it does. And, then to descend to a still lower depth, it argues from the very Scriptures, and proves to its own satisfaction, and the easement of its own benumbed conscience, that this is the very condition of soul that God desires and has planned His people to enjoy.

Yes; there is something higher up than this. But how much higher? In our dissatisfaction with this state of things we must not rebound too far and make the standard of a possible ascent too high. How much higher up? Can a question be more interesting? Can a question be more important than that which asks how much of holiness, and power, and victory, and God, can be possessed down here in this very present world. Oh, what books have been written, what sermons have been preached, what hymns have been sung to describe and make plain to us the possible attainments of the heavenly state. Every hour of every day multitudes are carried away with ecstatic expectation of what they are going to see and hear, and feel, and be, on the other side of Jordan. But are there not wonderful visions, and revelations, and signs, and feelings, and capacities, on this side of Jordan, that are worth inquiring about. In the kingdom of glory, above the stars, no doubt it will be grand beyond conception; but, short of that, down here in this lightly appreciated kingdom of grace there is a great deal that is well worth possessing, a very "kingdom of heaven" that is worth acquiring though it do require some force to take it. You may have to wait a few years before you are summoned to the fourth heaven; meanwhile, perhaps the first, or the second, or the third heaven may have some charms for you. Anyway many of our readers will readily confess that there are conditions, and experiences, and enjoyments, and revelations, and baptisms, far exceeding in height, and length, and depth, and breadth, anything they at present know and feel and possess. Let us inquire concerning them. Don't be afraid, dear reader, we are not going off into any intricate and puzzling theological disquisition; we simply propose to present a few particulars of this higher up religion, and to point out the shortest and easiest, nay, the only method of getting up into it.

We will begin with cautions. Perhaps we ought to do, although we are not quite sure about it. We used to think we ought always carefully to guard ourselves from being misunderstood, when we came to talk about how much grace can be had down here, in order to prevent people believing *too much* and aiming *too high.* But really when we find almost everybody who talks or writes about gracious gifts, and powers, and privileges, warning everybody else that they are not to expect too much, that God cannot save from this evil or bring them into that good, we are led to doubt whether we ought not to throw caution and prudence overboard, and go in for the thing as God does, for there is very little caution and prudence (so called) in God's book and plan. However, we will give a caution or two in the proper orthodox manner.

AND HERE LET ME SAY THAT THERE IS NO PLACE IN CHRISTIAN EXPERIENCE SO HIGH UP AS TO BE

BEYOND THE SIGHT AND REACH AND TEMPTING POWER OF THE DEVIL. You cannot get out of the sound of his voice, nor from within the range of his strong bow, and of his poisoned-barbed arrows. Though you do go to live in Hallelujah Terrace, on the right-hand side of Thy-will-be-done Street, which is a goodly street of very pleasant situation that runs along the brow of Full Salvation Hill, leading straight up to the pearly gates that open on to the Golden City. Though you should be enabled by divine grace thus to fix your abode on high, Satan will find you out, write down the number of your dwelling in his memorandum-book, and will come and go thither far more frequently and with far more determination than he does now you reside in that dark, damp, and doleful Grumbling Alley which runs directly out of Doubting Street, in the parish of Self Indulgence. Get higher up, a very long way higher up, by all means; God and angels, your own peace, and every possibility of usefulness urge you to get higher up; but remember that the Devil will follow and harass you there even more than he does in the low lands, where now, perchance, you dwell.

Get higher up, and you will not only present a better mark for the enemy, but be, in his estimation, better worth while shooting at, nay, he will find a new necessity for shooting at you. Satan pays little heed to those who, while professing godliness, are all the time destitute of its power. He has no need to trouble himself with and about such, seeing they could not very well serve his purpose better. And next to these are those who, having a measure of grace, are still only partially renewed, who, along with undeniable evidence of a work of grace, manifest, in words, temper, and habits equally undeniable evidence of the continued existence of much remaining evil in the soul. These live in a very mixed life, and consequently a life of both good and evil influences. Alas, the evil is often greater than the good ; but only let such come up to this higher platform, let them wash their robes and make them *white*, let them get emptied of self and sin, be made pure in heart, and come to know the love of Christ which passeth knowledge, and be filled with all the fulness of God, and then their lives will be so striking a testimony for God, and their power with God and man will be such that the Devil will feel called upon, nay, compelled, in the interests of his kingdom and glory, to attack them with all his might, which he will most assuredly do, either as a roaring lion or an angel of light, as he may judge most likely to succeed. But attack them he will.

But, thank God! there is provision made for victory. No weapon formed against faithful, obedient, believing souls shall prosper. There are three sources of temptation, and only three, namely, *the world*, *the flesh*, and *the devil*. Provision is made in the scheme of redemption for our overcoming each of these three great enemies.

First source of temptation, The World, of which the Holy Spirit says, "This is the victory that overcometh the world, even your faith."

Secondly, The Flesh, of which the Holy Ghost says, "If ye walk in the spirit, ye shall not fulfil the lusts of the flesh."

Thirdly, The Devil, of which also the Holy Ghost says, "The shield of faith shall quench all the fiery darts of the wicked one."

It must be so. Although God allows the attack, he has made arrangements for its defeat. Victory is not only a possibility, but a probability, and may, thank God! be made a dead certainty. Fight on! then, my comrades; and as you fight you may sing—

What though a thousand hosts engage
  A thousand worlds my soul to shake?
I have a shield shall quell their rage,
  And drive the alien armies back.
Pourtrayed, it bears a bleeding Lamb.
I dare believe in Jesu's name.

The War Cry, No. 4.—JAN. 17, 1880.

A HIGHER UP RELIGION.

BY THE GENERAL.

II.

OUR theme is holiness. We speak to those who hunger and thirst after righteousness. You are the children of God. You have passed from death unto life. Your sins are forgiven you, and *you know it*. A great change has passed over you. Once you were the willing slave of sin. Sin in some form reigned over you, but the Saviour came, and He brought not only pardon but liberty. You were made free. You are free to-day. Hallelujah! Still, the work of deliverance is not complete. True, the absolute triumphing reign of evil in your soul has come to an end, but it is still there. The Philistine still dwells in the land, and the enemies who once had it all their own way still disturb your peace. At times they overcome you, bring you into condemnation, and threaten totally to subdue and bring you again into bondage. We need not enumerate those enemies. You know them only too well,—anger, malice, pride, envy, lust, and the like. All the land, that is, all your heart and life was once their own, and fain would they have it back again. You have had many a fight with them, and, I fear, suffered many a defeat, which defeats have had to be followed by tears of bitter repentance and fresh applications to the cleansing-blood. Oh, ten thousand thanks for the continued efficacy of the crimson fountain, and the never-failing willingness of Jehovah to forgive.

His mercy, indeed, to those who seek it endureth for ever. And the next best thing to not stumbling and falling down is, I suppose, to get up again, and the next best thing to not falling into sin is to repent and seek forgiveness. But is there no other way? Yes, we show you another and a more excellent way. It is according to God's plan and nature to forgive sin, but it is none the less according to His plan and nature to save from sinning. He is able to keep us from falling, and He is able to make us stand, and not only to stand but to run and not be weary, to walk and not faint. Bless His dear name. For is not His name called Jesus? And was not that name, which signifies deliverance, given to Him because He should save His people from their sins. Yes, He saves from sin down here, in this very evil world; He saves to the uttermost; He saves fully; He saves, He saves to-day.

This is the experience, dear reader, we want to set before you, and to prevent misunderstanding we pursue the line of remark started last week. We left off at the statement *that there was no position so exalted down here as to free us from temptation.* Adam and Eve were tempted, and, beyond controversy, they were without sin. Jesus Christ knew no sin, and yet Satan attacked Him, and haunted and followed Him as perhaps, he never attacked and haunted and followed any other being, and that just because He was the best and holiest and most Godlike being that ever walked the earth. The devil saw Him and hated Him, perhaps as he had never hated a being before. Hence, he must either have flown from Him or flown at Him. He flew at Him, but only to be hurled back again and trampled upon and bruised. If you are a good copy of your Example, your Original, he will see the resemblance, see it before anyone else, and he will feel something of the old hatred and fly at you. But as He, your Master, overcame, so may you, so shall you, if you are a faithful soldier, and you shall sit down with Him on His throne even as He has sat down on His Father's throne. But remember that resemblance to Christ, rather than saving you from temptation, will only the more certainly bring it upon you.

THIS IS NOT AN EXPERIENCE SO HIGH UP THAT YOU WILL BE SAVED FROM INFIRMITIES.—We came into the world with minds and bodies diseased and deranged as the result of sin. Our fathers, a good way back, have eaten sour grapes, and the children's teeth have been set upon an edge. We reap—in our imperfect memories and damaged perceptions and emaciated and diseased bodies—the result of their transgressions and also of our own. Hence, mentally, we are prone to make mistakes, all sorts of mistakes; while, bodily, the worship we give and the service we render to the Great God of

Heaven is marred and disfigured. But these infirmities cannot justly be accounted sins. I cannot condemn myself for what I cannot help. If I have a crook in my leg or a twist in my eye, no power can make me blame myself for my limping gait or my defective vision. They are infirmities and not sins —infirmities which render my service all imperfect contrasted with the pure service of perfect beings, but which imperfection is more than met and covered by the all-atoning sacrifice of my Saviour.

The requirements our loving Father makes upon his children are graduated to their ability. If I am strong I must serve with my strength, if I am weak, according to my weakness. If I am wise I must serve with my wisdom, if I am ignorant according to the little light I possess. If I have ten talents I must use every one of them, if I have only one that one must be made the most of for His glory and the good of souls. "Thou shalt love the Lord thy God with *all* thy heart." Therefore, whether it be a big heart or a little heart, so that it be laid on the altar and filled with His love; whether in this sense it be a perfect or an imperfect heart, He will be content. The work may be very imperfect, but if the eye has been single and the intention pure, if the worker has been perfectly offered and sprinkled and accepted, God will be pleased and satisfied, and say, amidst the plaudits of angels, "Well done, thou good and faithful servant."

The War Cry, No. 12.—MARCH 13, 1880.

A HIGHER UP RELIGION.

BY THE GENERAL.

III.

HOW FAR CAN I BE SAVED?

THIS is a question, as we have already intimated, of thrilling interest to every really converted soul. Hunger and thirst after all inward and outward rightness with God and before Him is *natural* to the spiritual man. And the possibility of complete deliverance must, whatever be his opinion, interest him, and deserve his most careful attention.

Can I be saved from sinning and from sin *here?* I know, you know, we all know, that we shall have deliverance there, in the new heavens and the new earth, but what about this very earth in which we are compelled to live for the present, can I love God with all my heart here in this town, in this house? Aye, in this poor body, with all its aches, and pains, and infirmities, with devils tempting me and men opposing me, and the mighty work of winning souls to Jesus on my hands, is it my Father's good pleasure to give me NOW that inner hidden kingdom of righteousness, peace, and joy in the Holy Ghost? That is the question; and that is a question of surpassing importance to every redeemed soul whose eyes shall rest on this paper.

IT MEANS HAPPINESS! Sin is the great evil of your existence. Perhaps you have thought otherwise. The Devil's great interest is to delude you by making you feel that your happiness is dependent on your circumstances. You used to think so in an unsaved state. You said then, if you could only secure some form or other of earthly treasure you should be blessed. And now, you say, with Christ *and something else* you will be happy. Give me *this* or *that and Jesus,* and it shall be all right. But it was not so then, and it is not so now. God is your great good. You were made to enjoy Him. He, and He only, can fill and satisfy your soul. Sin separated you from God before conversion, and now sin dulls your senses and clouds your vision, and prevents God manifesting Himself in all His glorious power within you.

Peter told the Jews that God, having raised up His Son Jesus, had sent Him to bless them. But how? By destroying the Roman yoke, and making them again a great, free, powerful nation? No! By the completion of their beautiful temple, and the revival, in all its pomp and magnificence, of that temple's ritual and service? No! By sending them trade, and commerce, and plenty, and health, and friendships, and all the desired relationships of family life? No? How then? Oh, Hallelujah! By turning every one of them away from his iniquities. That was the Lord's plan for making the Jews blessed; but they would not have it, and rejected it and Him who brought it, and the great bulk of them clung to their iniquity, although it was the deadly poison which drank up their life's joy, and shut out from them the great Healer, and Saviour, and Joy Giver, and died and were damned in it. And so with you, dear reader. God has sent Jesus to you on the same heavenly, benevolent errand. He comes to your heart to bless, and gladden, and satisfy; but he comes to do it in this very way. *He cannot do it* in *any other*, and that is by turning you away from your iniquities. They are the asps whose venom poisons the springs of gladness in your soul. He has come to destroy them, the works of the devil,—all of them, big and little; and the little—if any of them can with propriety be so called—no less than the big; to destroy them root and branch, fruit and flower, and leaves and branches, and stem and root,—the whole Upas tree must go! His mission to you,—His mission of mercy, and blood, and sacrifice,—is to make an end—a complete end—of sin in your soul. So shall ye have peace and abiding joy, and in no other way.

IT MEANS USEFULNESS. You want to be of some service to the Master, and to your brethren, and to poor perishing sinners. Very good. This, too, is a never absent instinct of a divine nature. To win souls to Christ, and to nurse and strengthen them when they are won. To be a saviour of men. Hallelujah. You are such in some measure already. You have His spirit, and are ever and anon about His business. But you are feeble and inconstant.

The fire burns low, and often seems ready to expire. It takes you almost all your time to keep yourself saved. Well, you want a higher up religion. You need to be holy, because holiness means strength, and faithfulness, and power. It removes doubts by bringing in assurance of personal salvation, and doubts, you know, mean always weakness; and it also removes all the hindrances to perpetual indwelling of Jehovah. As sin goes out, God comes in; and with Christ fully dwelling in the vessel, in the temple, in the body, you will be fully equipped and qualified for every good work. Holiness means usefulness. Come, then, let us pursue this interesting and important inquiry. How far can God save from sin here? And we are sure our readers will agree with us—at least, we hope they will—when we say that this question can only be satisfactorily answered by hearing what the Lord says on the subject; and, having listened to the Scriptures, you may then with propriety and advantage listen to the testimony of those who boldly profess to have an experience on the subject.

What says the Word of the Lord? What people say—whether they be learned or unlearned, official or unofficial, or anything else—if they speak not in harmony with the direct and plain teaching of the Word of God, they speak not the truth on this subject, whatever they may do on any other. And as the opinions of other men are not our standard, neither are their lives. If A and B say I cannot be saved from sinning,—if they say I must go on in unbelief, and unfaithfulness, and evil tempers, unto the end of my earthly days; if they say I cannot love God with all my heart, and be loyal with simple obedience to my heavenly King,—I ask A and B for their authority; and if they confess that, after some two or three disjointed, misapprehended texts of Scripture, they rely upon the fact that this unholy, inconsistent, spirit-grieving life is the common confessed experience of the bulk of Christians, and therefore nothing better is possible to me,—I reject their authority. I won't accept the backsliding experience of any number of people as the standard of religious attainment for me. It is not what men are, but what God wants them to be; not what they actually possess and enjoy of purity, and peace, and power, but what Christ, the blessed Christ, with his agony and blood bought for them; what the Father freely offers, and what the pleading, long-suffering Holy Spirit waits to bestow. If I live at Ephesus, am I to conclude that it is impossible for me to keep my first love with its self-consuming, soul-saving power? or if my lot is cast in Laodicea, am I to teach that it is the right and acceptable thing before God and men not to be enthusiastic, not to be eaten up with the zeal of God's house, not to be burning hot; but to be miserably, contemptibly lukewarm in His service?

Oh, my brethren, my comrades in The Salvation Army, to you I write, Beware of this measuring yourselves with yourselves. It is not wise. Endless loss, and sorrow, and backsliding have been caused by it,—contenting ourselves with being as good as other people. And yet many will do it, no matter how warned or cautioned they may be; and therefore let us hurry up to the high levels of attainment, so that instead of dragging men down to Ephesus and Laodicea we may lift them up to Mount Beulah, and draw them on to that blessed highway, the highway of holiness.

The War Cry, No. 23.—May 29, 1880.

A HIGHER UP RELIGION.

By THE GENERAL.

VIII.

THE DESTRUCTIBILITY OF SIN.

We return to our theme. Our war is with sin. Here we are sure we are one in plan and purpose with Jehovah. About this we have no hesitation. Sin is the great evil He wants utterly to destroy. For this purpose the Son of God was manifested that He might destroy the works of the Devil. The plan is revealed in The Book—"If we confess our sins, He is faithful and just to forgive us our sins, and TO CLEANSE US FROM ALL UNRIGHTEOUSNESS."

What is sin? Sin is the transgression of the law, and all unrighteousness (all unrightness) is sin. Where is sin? It has a lodging-place, unfortunately, in this otherwise beautiful and happy world. But where does it abide here? Not in the material part of it. Not in the mountains and oceans and plains and rivers; they are sinless. Not in the animal world. The birds and beasts have no condemnation: they never transgressed the law of their Maker. Sin has its abode in the heart of man. Out of the heart of man—the favourite of heaven—alas! proceedeth all evil things. Here is the source and dwelling-place of the traitor. This is the citadel possessed by the enemy, and against this stronghold God levels his guns. From hence the foe must be dislodged. But is this possible? Can he be got out of this centre, so that when Satan cometh he shall find nothing of his own—nothing there in harmony with his black rebellious nature? Hallelujah! We believe it can be done. All things are possible with God, and all things are possible to him that believeth. Let us see.

Now let it be known, as it already will have been, we suppose, by those who have read the former papers of this series, that we are writing for simple uneducated people—people not only untaught in theological and biblical schools, but in all other kinds of schools, and that, therefore, we must strive in the plainest language and the most homely illustrations to make ourselves understood.

We have talked about God destroying sin out of the soul: putting it away and keeping it away, and so, beautifully uniting the heart to fear, and love, and serve Him. No Philistines left in the land, neither in the hill country, nor the valleys. The sovereignty and rule of Jehovah acknowledged and obeyed from the centre to the circumference. Peace in all the borders of the soul: devils outside, and all manner of devilish people, and, consequently, all manner of storms and miseries too; but inside, the peace of God which passeth understanding, keeping the heart and mind from sin, and constituting verily, verily, a well of water springing up unto eternal life.

About this destruction of sin there is much darkness and confusion, and we do not profess to be able to make it all plain. All we hope to do is to help souls so to close with their Saviour that He shall answer, through their hearts, their puzzling questions, and remove their doubts, by completely satisfying that hunger of soul out of which so many doubts and puzzling questions spring.

We were talking about the destruction of sin. This is what we want to make clear. We hate sin. That is the devil we want ejecting from our hearts. Every real child of God has a loathing of evil and an inward indestructible longing to have no fellowship or community whatever with the unfruitful works of darkness, and it is only the most mistaken and misguided teaching, we think, that can induce any of the children of God to accept with any degree of contentment the doctrine that there is a necessity to sin and to be sinful to the end of the chapter.

Now, so far as we know, there are four different theories or opinions held with respect to the indwelling of sin, and the power and purpose of God to destroy it in this life.

I. THERE IS THE TWO NATURE THEORY, which says that at conversion there is no actual change wrought in the soul of the sinner, but that there is engrafted in him, alongside the old nature, a new nature; which new nature is divine, or, as it has been stated, is a part of the divine nature. That side by side these two natures remain till death do them part, the one antagonistic to the other, in perpetual conflict—unalterable, indestructible—until the skeleton hand of death severs them and ends the strife, the good nature incapable of sin, the bad nature incapable of holiness. Where the bad nature resides, whether in the flesh or in the spirit, there is some confusion. Some think the evil is in the flesh, that is, in the bones, and sinews, and blood; others think it is an essential part of the mind. But with this we stay not to inquire. To our minds there are insuperable difficulties in the view; it appears as irrational as unscriptural. To say nothing else it is a gloomy view, and on the face of it seems to render impossible the fulfilment of all the blessed injunctions of the Bible, and all the inward yearnings of a man's new heavenly spirit after a glad, and a holy, and a victorious life. But there it is: that is the view, and conviction, and teaching of many. That as bad and black, aye, even as bad and black as in my unconverted days, my old heart remains, only that alongside of it there has come into my soul a new, heavenly, holy, divine nature, which may be the master of the evil nature at times, which may always be the master, but it is not to be expected, and that fighting and conflicting, these two must go forward till death.

Nay, there are, it occurs to us while we write, many who would say that the better nature is and must be very largely, nay, mostly be in subjection to the worse; that Paul teaches this in the seventh of Romans; that the good things which the new and better nature WOULD do, those the old evil nature will NOT allow it to do; and the evil things which the new and better nature WOULD NOT do, those the old and evil nature COMPELS it to do, and that there is no help for it.

II.—THE SECOND IS THE GRADUAL EXTINCTION THEORY. This view contends that at conversion a radical change is made in the soul in the direction of sanctification, that power is given over sin, which power is gradually increased day by day, but that sin still remains, although enfeebled and stunted, growing more and more helpless, only receiving the finishing stroke at death; that sanctification is a growth, a perpetual growth, but not completed till the final moment of existence. A great difficulty about this theory is that it contradicts so much that one sees and knows daily in the ordinary experience of believers. How few there are—at least we have come across very few, if any—who have professed to a life of progress in goodness. The great bulk of the Lord's children, we should think, if they spoke the truth, would have to say just the contrary. That after years of experience and opportunity they are not as much separated from evil, and as fully given up to God and the salvation of souls as when they first believed. We are afraid that the great bulk of believers have to repent and do their first works before they can go into Heaven, which, doubtless, many do at its very gates. This is only one difficulty in the way of this opinion, but we shall perhaps have occasion to notice it again further on in these papers.

III.—THE THIRD THEORY TEACHES THE COMPLETE SUBORDINATION OF THE OLD NATURE. This is a modification of the first, and, as held by many, goes almost as far, practically, as we do ourselves. It says that God will not, does not, destroy the old nature; nevertheless, He will, in answer to faith, that is, on the compliance with certain conditions, put the old nature into the place of death, REDUCE IT TO IMPOTENCE, MAKE IT HELPLESS—a sort of MUMMY, still there but POWERLESS, still there till death utterly destroys it. Now, our chief difficulty with this view is that it sounds unnatural, mystical, and puzzling to simple, wayfaring people, and so directly antagonistic to those clear deliverances of the Bible, which, without the slightest reservation, sound out and declare God's good pleasure to give a CLEAN HEART, to destroy sin and the works of the Devil, to CLEANSE FROM ALL IDOLS, and RENEW RIGHT HEARTS and SPIRITS within those of His people who want them, who will come out from among the ungodly and touch not the unclean thing.

And, without dwelling here, we have one great difficulty with all these theories, and that is that they all make death a sort of Deliverer and Saviour, putting him, the grim monster, into the place of the blessed Jesus, whose great and glorious prerogative it is to save His people not only from Hell, but from sin.

IV.—THE FOURTH IS THE EXTINCTION THEORY.—That is the view we have endeavoured to inculcate in these papers—that in whatever part of our nature sin has its seat—and it is not worth wasting a word to prove that there is by nature and practice a deceitful and unclean heart in man, out of which proceed evil thoughts, words and deeds, this theory declares that God can destroy it, that He does destroy it, when trusted to do so. That a soul may go to Him full of confidence that his request will be granted as much so when he asks for a clean heart as when he asks for the pardon of his sins.

And why should this be thought in any way surprising? Is it not exactly what we might have expected could we by any means have anticipated the circumstances and efforts of God to save us? Perceiving and realising the evil and degradation, and pollution of sin, should we not have calculated that, after pardoning us, all His desires would have turned in the direction of delivering us out of the hand of the enemies of our peace and usefulness, the plagues of our hearts, the evils still existing within us, and of doing it as soon as possible. Nay, is it not just what we would do for men and women were we in His place? With the little knowledge we have of the deadly, hateful, blighting, damning nature of sin, would we not, were we on that high throne of power, and authority, and love, seek to destroy those tendencies that are the mainspring and source of all the sin and misery of which we have any knowledge whatever?

My brethren and comrades, come this way. Let us cease from our reasonings. God, as we have already remarked, will answer your difficulties in the depths of your soul, if you will let Him. Make Him your Teacher. TRY AND PROVE HIM, and see if He will not do for you far more exceeding and abundantly above all that you ask or think. That is, He will exceed all that you ask expecting, and He will exceed all that you think He can do for and in and by you. Try Him honestly and with all your heart and in His own way, and send your experience along to the Editor of "THE WAR CRY" that it may be an encouragement for others to go and do likewise. Amen.

The War Cry, No. 27.—JUNE. 26, 1880.

A HIGHER UP RELIGION.

BY THE GENERAL.

IX.

DELIVERANCE FROM SIN.

WE cannot help remarking, with satisfaction and gratitude, the increasing attention that is being given to the topic of which we write. In and out of the Army, by old converts no less than new ones, the inquiry is being anxiously made—Is it so? Is there deliverance for me from my heart plagues, my inward enemies; is it true? Can it possibly be true that I can here, on earth, not only cease from grieving my Saviour but have grace to enable me always to do the things that are pleasing in His sight. And we don't wonder in the least at this spirit of interest and inquiry. The topic once started is certain to arrest the attention, and command the sympathy of sincere souls. In the depths of every spiritual nature there is a yearning—an upward reaching after the fullest possible obedience and conformity to the Divine will—a hungering and thirsting after righteousness that can only be met and satisfied by the Divine fulness. This is not only a fruit but a sign of the possession of true saving grace. The man who does not realize this longing after entire holiness has good reason, we think, to fear that he has not been made a partaker of the Divine nature. The pious Dr. Doddridge says, "To allow yourself deliberately to sit down, satisfied with any imperfect attainments in religion, and to look upon a more confirmed and improved state of it as what you do not desire, nay, as what you secretly resolve that you will not pursue, is one of the most fatal signs we can well imagine, that you are an entire stranger to the first principles of it." And the Holy Ghost says, by the Apostle John, "Every one that hath this hope in Him purifieth himself even as He is pure."

No wonder, then, that hearts influenced and impressed with heavenly love should be stirred with the tidings of a full salvation, should be moved when the spies come along with the wonderful tidings of the Canaan land of perfect love, flowing with the milk and honey of peace and joy. Especially when the figs and grapes and pomegranates in the shape of the ungainsayable testimonies of saved and sanctified, happy, heavenly people, are spread out before them. Oh! it is then a perfectly natural response for sincere and earnest souls to cry out, "Let us also go over Jordan and secure for ourselves this Divine and heavenly country."

Now, this is just what might have been expected. To look is to love, and to love is to long after and seek, and, thank God, to seek is to obtain, for verily,

verily it has been said, "Ask, and it shall be given you; seek, and ye shall find; knock, and it shall be opened unto you; for EVERY ONE THAT ASKETH RECEIVETH, and he that SEEKETH FINDETH, and to him that KNOCKETH it shall be OPENED."

Now, is it not always just at the point where the soul fully decides to attempt the higher and holier walks of religious enjoyment and usefulness that Satan comes in with his long list of difficulties and impossibilities? As the Israelites were affrighted with stories about the impassable walls of the cities, and the lofty stature and grim fierceness and terrible weapons of the Canaanites, at the very verge of their inheritance, just so multitudes of the Lord's children of later times have been met and terrified on the borders of another and far brighter land of promise with difficulties—difficulties material, difficulties human, and, alas, difficulties professedly Divine.

My comrades, my brethren, we have already granted, and we grant again, that there are difficulties, stupendous difficulties, difficulties in the shape of the world, the flesh. and the devil, difficulties in the people of God, and difficulties, at first sight, in the very book of God itself; but, as difficulties vanished when these sons of Abraham of old boldly faced them, in the name and strength of the loving Jehovah, so, ye sons of believing Abraham, shall these difficulties, whether diabolic, human, or Divine vanish before you, when you leave the wilderness, cross the Jordan of your unbelief, and boldly enter upon the inheritance purchased and promised, and held out to you.

FOR ARE NOT ALL THINGS POSSIBLE TO HIM THAT BELIEVETH?

Now, we will, as far as in us lies, dispose of these difficulties. And we think we shall, perhaps, meet these negatives, and doubts, and fearfulnesses by showing, from the Holy Scriptures, that it is our Father's good pleasure to give us this inward kingdom of righteousness, and peace, and joy, and to give it us now. And we will take—

I. THE ARGUMENT FROM SCRIPTURE.

Now, in entering upon this part of our subject, we are bewildered with the profusion of proof. It is difficult to make a selection of texts. The whole Bible, in spirit and in letter, seems to say "Be ye holy." Ask yourself, dear reader, What does this Book teach me? What sort of a saint does this Book show me I ought to be? We are afraid multitudes of people read their Bibles in an abstract sort of way, to find out what God has done in the past for the world, or what he is going to do with it, or, at most, what good things He has to bestow upon them in the future, rather than to inquire, which must be the most important of all, What kind of a saint does this book show me I ought to be? and what sort of service ought I to render to God and my fellow men? My brother, take your Bible and use it as a glass, as a double glass, which it most certainly is. A glass which, on one side, will reveal to you WHAT YOU ARE, and on the other side will, with equal fidelity, show you WHAT YOU OUGHT TO BE.

Let us take a glance at it. And with regard to

the passages we quote, let us say that, in common with all the practical portions of this book, our main duty is to accept the surface meaning of the text. If there is a plain, natural meaning apparent at first sight in the passages, a meaning which is in accordance with the general spirit and purpose of the whole book, you are not to go away to find some fanciful interpretation, in order to make it square with your own experience or theories or theologies, or anything else, but to take that plain surface meaning and act upon it. The Bible is intended to be its own interpreter, and, like the religion which it proclaims, is ordinarily easily understood by the plainest and most unlettered of men; fools and wayfaring men do not err herein. Mainly all the muddles and heresies of the ages gone by, and the ages present, have come from heads full of learning and genius. Don't be scared by what doctors of divinity may say, however humble and ignorant of earthly learning and theories you may be. Get down low at Jesus' feet. Read your Bibles there. Cry continually for the direct illumination of the Holy Ghost, and you shall verily be led into all needed truth. In this spirit we direct you to the following scriptures, and, that we may have some form in our quotations, we remark—

1st.—That the Bible commands saints to live without sin. We begin with God's injunction to Israel: "Hear, O Israel, thou shalt love the Lord thy God with all thy soul and with all thy might." "And now, Israel, what doth the Lord thy God require of thee but to fear the Lord thy God, to walk in His ways, and to love Him, and to serve the Lord thy God with all thy heart and with all thy soul, to keep the Commandments of the Lord thy God and His statutes, which I command thee this day for thy good."—Deut. vi. 5; x. 12, 13. This command, with slight variation of words, was repeated by the Saviour, when He said, "Thou shalt love the Lord thy God with all thy heart, and with all thy soul, and with all thy mind, and with all thy strength, and thy neighbour as thyself.—Luke x. 27.

Now we take these commands to carry with them all we ask for. They are nothing more nor less than the soul loving God supremely, and making His glory and the accomplishment of His purposes the supreme end of existence. And this must be done with all the ability possessed.

If love be the fulfilling of the law, and if the soul loves to the utmost of its powers—whether these powers are great or little—then that soul must fulfil the law, and, while so doing, does not grieve God, in other words, does not sin. And this is what God requires, and the requirement must carry with it the ability to obey. God is not a hard master. He does not reap where He has not sown, nor gather where He has not strawed. He does not ask His people to make bricks without straw. All these commands, like the promises, are yea and amen in Christ Jesus, seeing that there is always the implied willingness of God to supply sufficient grace to enable those who receive them to comply with what is enjoined. Look up, my brother, you want to love God with all your heart, present yourself before God as He has directed, and he will supply ABUNDANCE OF GRACE. Gird up the loins of your mind and present yourself for the glorious work of PERFECT LOVE. Don't be affrighted by the evil reports of half-hearted brethren, or by the memories of your own past failures. You have often heard the story of the coloured brother, who said, in allusion to needed strength for divinely-appointed duty: If God commanded me to jump through that stone wall, my duty would be to jump; it would be God's business to see I went through. And whatever God does command, if you will consecrate yourself to the doing thereof, depending on His Holy Spirit for ability, you shall surely prove, and in your own soul exemplify the sufficiency of His power to carry you through. For, has He not said, who cannot lie, "My grace is SUFFICIENT for thee?" Believe and obey and the victory shall be yours.

The War Cry, No. 32.—July 31, 1880.

A HIGHER UP RELIGION.

By THE GENERAL.

X.

DELIVERANCE FROM SIN PROMISED.

In our last paper we referred to certain Scriptures in which God commands, in the most positive and direct manner, His people to be holy, that is, to live without sin. We propose now to quote a few texts as specimens of numbers in the Bible, in which the blessing of holiness is as definitely and as distinctly promised. We begin with Deut. xxx. 6, "And the Lord thy God will circumcise thine heart, and the heart of thy seed to love the Lord thy God with all thine heart and with all thy soul, that thou mayest live." Now, here God directly promises just what the law requires, all the grace and strength needed to enable the soul to comply with the commands before quoted, and are here promised. To love God with all thy heart implies also the love of our neighbour, and love is the fulfilling of the law. It cannot be controverted that this promise was intended to be fulfilled in this life. When the

Israelites first received it, they regarded it as intended for fulfilment in them then and there. And if for them, why not for us? why not for me? Can anyone find any satisfactory reason why God should not, according to this promise, so change and sanctify my nature that I should love Him with all my heart, and you also, dear reader? Amen. Even so, Come, Lord Jesus.

Again, take Exekiel xxxvi. 25-27, "Then will I sprinkle clear water upon you, and ye shall be clean from all your filthiness, and from all your idols will I cleanse you. A new heart also will I give you, and a new spirit will I put within you; and I will take away the stony heart out of your flesh, and I will give you a heart of flesh. And I will put My Spirit within you and cause you to walk in My statutes, and ye shall keep My judgments and do them." Now, if this passage does not contain a promise of entire sanctification, of complete deliverance from sin, and of the ability to comply with all the requirements God seeks from us, I am at a loss to know what it means. Of course, it can be reasoned away and made of none effect. But so can any other text in the Bible, and what remains to us then? But we affirm this cannot be done without violating the rules of fair and honest interpretation. Let us look at it. What does God here engage to do for His people?

1. To make you clean by the power of the Holy Ghost. Then will I sprinkle clean water (the Spirit) upon you, and you shall be clean. Now, God here says, *you shall be clean.* He knows when a heart is clean, and He

declares it shall be done. Who shall say it *shall not.*

2. To cleanse you from all your filthiness and from all your idols. Not from half, three parts, seven-eighths, but from *all.* Who is going to controvert this, and say all only means part; or that the filthiness and the idols shall be so removed as that a part, a little part, shall be left; or that all the filthiness shall not be entirely removed, but covered up and left behind somewhere as a sort of hotbed, in which the seeds of temptation may fructify, and take root, and spring up? No, the words used by the Holy Ghost are simple and understandable. He says, "From *all* your filthiness and from *all* your idols will I cleanse you."

3. He promises a new heart and a new spirit. That is, a heart and spirit altogether new, with no part of the old, unbelieving, treacherous, sinful heart remaining; and he will take away the stony heart, and give a heart of flesh; that is, he will remove the heart that was so unsympathetic with the Divine and spiritual things, and give a new heart all tender and responsive to the interests of Christ and the Kingdom.

4. He will ensure the permanence of this by the indwelling of the Spirit, which shall be the power that worketh within us. I will put My Spirit within you, and *cause* you to walk in My statutes, and you shall keep My judgments, and do them.

5. To whom is this promise made, and when are we to expect its fulfilment? We reply, without hesitation, to all those who comply with the conditions of *a full consecration* and *a hearty faith*, for we are expressly informed that God is no respecter of persons, and that all the promises of God are in him, yea, and in Him, Amen, to the Glory of God by us.

"And this was manifestly designed to apply to Christians under the new dispensation, rather than to the Jews under the old dispensation. The sprinkling of clean water, and the outpouring of the Spirit, seem plainly to indicate that the promise belonged more particularly to this than the old dispensation. It undeniably belongs to the same class of promises with that in Jeremiah xxxi. 31-34, Joel ii. 28, and many others, that manifestly looks forward to the gospel day, when they shall become due. As these promises have never been fulfilled in their extent and meaning, their complete fulfilment remains to be realised by Christians as a body. And those individuals, and that generation, will take possession of the blessing who understand, and believe, and appropriate them to their own case."

We give next the promise contained in 1 Thess. v. 23-24. "And the very God of peace sanctify you wholly; and I pray God your whole spirit and soul and body be preserved blameless unto the coming of our Lord Jesus Christ. Faithful is He that calleth you, who also will do it." On this let it be observed—

1. That it is admitted that sanctify signifies to

separate from sin, and to set apart for the service of God.

2. That the Holy Ghost here leads Paul to pray that the Thessalonians may be thus *wholly* or *entirely* separated from evil, and given up to doing the will of God.
3. That lest this should not be sufficiently explicit, he prays that the *whole* man—comprised of the spirit, soul, and body—may be preserved *blameless.*
4. To be *preserved* blameless implies *made* blameless, and to be *blameless* implies that nothing is done that is *blameworthy.*
5. And this blameless state was to be *permanent* —*to continue to the coming of our Lord Jesus Christ.*
6. And, further, it is expressly stated that God, who calls us to this holy state, is faithful to fulfil in us all needed grace for its accomplishment.

There are multitudes of other promises, all of which, with more or less distinctness, conveying the assurance that it is our Father's good pleasure to give to His people this kingdom of righteousness. Those we have mentioned, if there were not others, would alone suffice to prove this, and we pass on to show that

CHRIST PRAYED THAT HIS PEOPLE WOULD BE FULLY DELIVERED FROM SIN IN THIS LIFE.

Hear him. "I pray not that thou shouldst take them out of the world, but that Thou shouldst keep them from the *evil.*" He did not pray that they should be delivered from temptation, poverty, affliction, persecution, stripes, imprisonment, or a violent death. Nay, he assured them of these things as being most likely to happen; but he did pray that they might be kept from sin. They might suffer—He expected and foretold that they would have all manner of tribulations, and made provision for them; and arranged that all should work together for the good of faithful souls; but He prayed and desired that there should be no evil—no sin.

WE ARE TAUGHT AND ENCOURAGED IN THE NEW TESTAMENT TO PRAY FOR ENTIRE HOLINESS IN THIS LIFE. Christ taught his disciples, and through them He teaches us to pray for this state. Hear Him in a prayer, continually offered by all the saints of the living God throughout the earth. "Thy will be done on earth as it is in heaven." This prayer is intended and accepted as a model prayer, in substance if not in words, given by the lips of THE GREAT TEACHER. Thy will be done on EARTH as it is in *heaven*. What? THY WILL. Thy beautiful, benevolent, holy, sinless, heavenly will be done. By whom? By you, by me, by all My disciples. OUTWARDLY: in the house, in the shop, in the marketplace, on the sea, on the land, towards wife, husband, children, servants; master, neighbour; towards friends, and enemies, and strangers; towards all—Thy will be done. INWARDLY: in the inner world of thought, and feeling, and purpose. Thy will be done by me, through me, in me, *now*, to-morrow, always, and that as *willingly*, and as *entirely*, and as *thoroughly* as it is in heaven. That is neither more nor less than that I should be as thoroughly given up to doing God's good pleasure on earth as I shall be when I come to heaven. If it were possible that you could go into heaven the imperfect creature you are on the earth, to do His will, you would have to sing to Him, work for Him, love Him to the uttermost of your ability. He desires the same here, and when you thus render yourself up He will possess you, and dwell in you. And though a very imperfect doing and serving it may appear to others, still He will accept it. He who singled out and applauded the offered mites of the poor widow, seeing that she did in sympathy and charity what she could, will accept your service and be pleased with it, and say of it in the depths of your soul, as you hope to hear him say of it some day before assembled worlds, "Well done, thou good and faithful servant."

My comrades, instead of quibbling and cavilling about this or that command being too hard for you, the time has come for you to gird yourself with the mighty promise of your Almighty God, and go boldly and believingly forth, and obey. *Amen.*

The War Cry, No. 36.—Aug. 28, 1880.

HOW TO TEACH HOLINESS.

By COMMISSIONER RAILTON.

1. In order to make the meaning of sanctification clear to the mind it is necessary first of all to go to the very root of sin's disease, and let people see how it is that sin so plagues and distresses those who are born again of the Holy Ghost. Those who are only taught to look at that which is outward and manifest are not to be wondered at if they fail to see properly what they need, and what God can do for them, and therefore only seek after and get deliverance from the outward signs and manifestations of sin.

2. Take the greatest pains to show by Scripture and by all sorts of illustrations, how man's nature has become, through the fall, so corrupted as to be inclined towards evil, so that even when men are saved and become fully devoted to the service of God, their nature still leans in the direction of all that is opposed to His will, so that between the spirit and the flesh there is constant strife, each

struggling at every turn for mastery, and the spirit only too often crushed by the Devil and the world, assisted by the flesh. Describe this battle particularly, showing just what passes within at certain moments.

3. Point out the evidences of this depraved nature in the little child, and show how the very same selfish and other evil tendencies which are exhibited by the little ones are those which cause the inconsistencies and inward conflicts of the saved man.

Get all to see that it is no use trying to make the fruit of the tree good by care and pruning whilst there is a mixture in the nature of the tree, causing it to produce fruits of the two opposite kinds, but that the only sensible plan is to get the tree itself made altogether such as you wish its fruit to be.

4. Contrast the fruits of the flesh and those of the Spirit, making all understand that God just as absolutely requires that the fruits of the flesh should cease to grow and that those of the Spirit should be abundantly produced as if it were not natural to men to bring forth the one and not to bring forth the other.

From the conflict which all are conscious of upon this subject, and from the shame that is felt when the fruits of the flesh are made manifest, you can convince them that only the one sort of fruit should exist, and that they can never have a truly peaceful and happy life till this is the case.

5. The facts of their heart experience must greatly weigh with them all. All men desire to live at peace within; but the struggle, whilst the

heart is divided, is so violent and produces so great discomfort that everyone longs for ease. It is then that the prescription of any spiritual quack who offers a false peace is valued. It is for you to show how a real enduring peace can alone be had, by abolishing the force which was against the Lord altogether, and thus leaving the heart free to enjoy and to follow Him fully. Those who have been led into the enjoyment of a mere superficial peace by means of what is called a "moment by moment" faith, or "power over sin," cannot in many cases be shown how they have been misled until the breakdown of their system or their peace opens their eyes. Yet there are cases in which such persons become so painfully conscious of the effort to keep believing that they can be awakened to the fact that the peace they have is not the perfect peace of those whose minds are stayed not upon their own faith, but upon Him who bears up the world.

6. Explain, in general and in all particulars, the Righteousness of God. That it is ceaseless, certain, willing conformity in everything with His Will, which makes perfect service and perfect freedom, pressing, especially, the grand principle that the Will of God is to be done by me here, just as I shall do it in Heaven, and that my will is to be as fully united with Him therein now as hereafter.

7. Make everyone see that such a state of things can only be brought about and continued anywhere by His being enthroned as the actual, absolute and undisputed King. That His Will was not done in Heaven fully whilst Satan was there, and that

which hinders its perfect fulfilment in any heart is the fact that the Devil has some authority therein.

8. This will bring fresh assurance of God's will and power to cast out the producing cause of all evil from within, and so to take full, absolute and perfect possession of our whole being for Himself. The depraved condition of the heart is one of the works of the Devil, which Jesus came on purpose to destroy for ever.

9. Point out the fact that godliness, the being like God, is all through the Bible continually regarded as a possible state for men, and that whatever is not of God is classed together as ungodliness, whether it be murder or one evil thought. That everyone who is not godly is so far ungodly as they are unlike God, and that God can only have perfect fellowship with those who are living on His level of pure light and love. "But if we walk in the light, as He is in the light, we have fellowship one with another, and the blood of Jesus Christ His Son cleanseth us from all sin."—1 John i. 7.

This fact will show with what eagerness He must desire to make all men godly. Indeed, every consideration of Him, His character, position, power, authority, and glory, must convince anyone who will look at it, that God cannot be willing for His children to be kept in a state of partial division from, and opposition to, Himself.

10. Upon the other hand, dwell upon the purposes, powers, and acts of the Devil, and show how the existence of evil anywhere favours his plans, and its destruction defeats him. Describe his

triumph whenever any one of God's children is disgraced, or brought into difficulty or sorrow through sin, and show that those who do not receive all God intends for them aid Satan's cause.

11. In all your descriptions of holiness, be careful always to keep to the front the fact that what is meant is the separation for a person from everything including themselves and their all to God, so that they come as fully into His own possession as if they were in Heaven. It is, of course, one consequence of this that the holy person receives Heaven into himself.

But it is very necessary always to keep in mind that the benefit to the man is a consequence and a secondary matter, not the thing to be desired and sought after. The commonly received, selfish theory of holiness is, that it is the getting of Heaven or of God into your heart and life, and the disastrous result of this sort of teaching is, that men take advantage of that boundless generosity with which God does pour peace and blessing into their seeking souls, and yet make no suitable return.

Now, whatever those do who make holiness their speciality, who occupy all their speaking time and strength with it, and will scarcely stoop to what they call the lower work of saving men from Hell, remember that our business is not firstly to seek men's happiness, but firstly to seek the kingdom of God, which will bring everything also. Therefore be ceaselessly on your guard against the subtle attempt of the great enemy to put man first, even at this critical point, and do your utmost to make all see that they are to seek for holiness not that they may be benefitted, but that God may have them entirely in His hands, to do His pleasure. Tell how for ages He has longed for a people who should be peculiarly His own, as utterly separated from sinners as Jesus was, and as perfectly in union with Himself in every way. Tell of all His weary waiting and disappointments, and of His long-suffering, patient love, and long that He may have the joy at last of seeing some such people.

12. Never lower the price of holiness. Point continually to the Cross, and show how real devotion to God must bring everyone into just such a position—suffering the loss of all things—a separation both from Heaven and earth; from Heaven, because they must lose much of even the quiet and spiritual enjoyment they might have amongst saints to plunge down amongst the lost; from earth, because they must be utterly hated "of all men;" and upon all this, instead of brightness and success, clouds and tempests and shame and apparent defeat. Bring people to that and you will get some real saints that God will delight in.

13. Impress continually upon those who love God the reality of the Judgment Day, as far as their own treatment is concerned. Amidst the general idea of being upon the right side, men lose sight of the more special descriptions of that day, which all point to the most careful and precise examination of each one as to what they have done and the exact distribution of reward and punishment according to men's deeds.

It is, alas! only too needful to remind the Lord's

people that He is not mocked, but that what a man sows that shall he reap. He that sows sparingly, we are expressly told, shall reap sparingly. Those who have largely sown to the flesh shall just to that extent reap corruption—shall see their works burned up with the King's indignation, and their names branded with irrecoverable shame for having so carelessly and unfaithfully served Him. God is no respecter of persons, and if He has marked out for ever the sins of Noah, of Abraham, of Moses, of David, and of Peter, let those who are so infinitely below all these in the general tenor of their lives expect a far more damaging exposure of all their impurities and faults before all mankind. It is evident that every saint is as surely preparing his own everlasting standing and destiny as every sinner. There will be many of God's ransomed ones who will meet Him not with joy but with grief. Press everyone as to how they would like to be suddenly brought into God's presence out of their present position—at home—at work—in the Army.

The War Cry, No. 51.—Dec. 11, 1880.

IS IT A DEFINITE WORK?

The doctrine of entire sanctification is not altogether of good repute in the world. Many deem it heretical nonsense. And it supposes a life of holiness and a cross of confession that are anything but agreeable to carnal minds and the current associations and customs of the day. From these facts, there is a natural tendency, in many convicted minds, to gloss some of its features, and even to give it the name of No-name.

But, beloved, beware! To be ashamed of Christ or His words is so shameful a transaction as to make the Lord ashamed of us, His followers, before the Father and the holy angels.

The experience is a definite experience. It is not mere growing in grace—that will come. It is not trying to do better, or be better, or feel better, but is a definite, distinct gift as clearly offered, and to be as clearly apprehended, and to be as clearly received and realised as pardon. Purity is not desiring to be pure.

The experience has definite bounds. It is not more justification. For if one sin is forgiven, all are forgiven. There is a sort of sanctification that is wrought at conversion. But even this is no sliding-scale affair. It is as distinct and well-defined in itself, and in its relation to entire sanctification, as the moon is in itself, and in its relation to the sun. That first sanctification is the superb work whereby we "become as little children." The heart—the great moral centre—is brought back to a spiritual state and relationship, exactly like that of a child to its father. All the guilt of a life of sin is sanctified away by the blood of Jesus.

Conviction for entire sanctification is a definite conviction for a definite work—in whatever form it may come, and however befogged the relation of the mind thereto. The heart clearly apprehends that it is burdened and needs to have something done for it.

The faith for entire sanctification is a definite thing. It is not that life of faith by which the converted person grows in the grace of which he is already possessed. Yet the two are not antagonists, but friends. They are not identical, or lost in each other. The faith for the second sanctification immediately follows a definite parting from sin, in all purpose and in all necessary outward form, and a complete devotement of every living power to God, for ever. When this faith is exercised, it is specific and complete. Its office is distinct and complete. It embodies a special, distinct and completed movement of the will. It is clean-cut, precise, perfect or entire trust, reliance of the heart on Jesus, by which it appropriates His all-sufficient blood for the distinct work that is in hand.

Then the answering voice of our dear Lord is raised in the seeker's behalf: "I will; be thou clean." Not partially clean, almost clean, but clean.

The work is instantly and perfectly done. It is immediately done, and well done. The heart is cleansed, entirely sanctified, and stands complete in love! Hallelujah!

Then the Spirit definitely testifies that the work of entire sanctification is wrought. It gives a new and intelligible testimony, not to some other work, nor to an indefinite work, but to the definite work of entire sanctification.

Now, let us for ever cease all jumbling. If we are sanctified wholly by the blood of Jesus, let us give a clear testimony to it. And be sure to honour God by definite work on the line of holiness. Justification, blessings, and works—everything—should be taught on the line of holiness.

The War Cry, No. 114.—Feb. 23, 1882.

MAN'S CHIEF GOOD.

Notes of an Address by Mrs. BOOTH, at Manchester, on Sunday Morning, January 29th, 1882.

As I look round this morning, the question presents itself to me: "Is there no way of showing people, —and especialy young people, before the terrible, trying, and harrowing experience of a lifetime, which it seems to take most people to learn it—is there no way of teaching people the great truth, the one end which God has in view in human life, yea, in allowing the race to continue, and in His dealings with the race all the way through, the one great lesson which we must learn if ever we get to Heaven, namely, That God is the Great Good, the one satisfying portion for the human soul?" Then, I said, "O Lord, do thou teach it to them. Reveal to them by Thy Spirit that Thou art the end for which they were created."

Satan has deluded the race by getting them to imagine that other ends, and things, and beings are the great good for which they were made. One young man sets his eyes on a beautiful young woman, loves her, and thinks that she will be his great good. She *will* be *a great good*, if she is a godly girl, but not THE great good for which he was made, and therefore if he stops short there, he will miss his mark, and God will perhaps have to take her away from him, to show him his mistake, and to lead him to seek his happiness in God.

Others think that getting on in the world, getting fame, reputation, or wealth will be *their* great good: they toil, and labour, and take a great deal more pains for it than will do them good, or satisfy them if they attain it. Oh! how many of these disappointed men I have talked to! Men whose life was almost gone, as their silver locks and tottering limbs testified, and, as they have looked back on their life, they have admitted, directly or indirectly, as I heard a man say a few days ago, "Yes, my life has been a *mistake*!" Such people try to satisfy their souls with that which can never satisfy them. Happy if, at last, like the prodigal, they find out their mistake, and turn to God before ALL IS LOST FOR EVER!

Others make their family their great good. They say, "I will make that boy this, and that girl the other;" but there is hardly a parent on earth can do with his children what he desires, and he finds that even his children are not his great good. I hear there are some of you that say "Amen" to that; but you will have bitterer things yet. God is bound to disappoint you, if He would save you, while you place your affections and ambitions on anything short of Himself. He *made you* FOR HIMSELF, and He will have you for Himself, or He will have to shut you up with the devil and his angels. The universe will only be divided into two parts at last,—those who will be *for* God, and those against Him. If you do not take Him for your great good now, you will be reckoned amongst those who are against Him then. Those beings that have affinities for each other gather together. If there were no God, and souls continue what they are, if after death your inclinations and dispositions are evil, you will go with the evil. The good will all go to the right hand, because right is right; and the bad will all go to the left, because wrong is wrong.

I have had rather a sharp tussle with the enemy this morning. As I was coming along in the bath chair I was taking myself to task, for I like to come to the foundation of things, and see where I am. It is fearfully possible for anyone to get wrong, for the Devil has a new trap for each day. I was pulling myself up before some questions which Satan had been thrusting before me. As I was reading in private this morning, this line struck me very forcibly—"Because thou hast trusted in *thy way*, and hast not trusted in the Lord," etc.

I said, "Oh, Lord! am I trusting in my way in anything?" Then I examined myself thus:—I said, "Supposing this were to happen so, and that were to happen so, all contrary to *my way*—to my poor judgment of what is the best. What would I do then?" and my heart said, "I would still trust in Thee, O Lord! Nay, if Thou should strip me of everything, and leave me naked and desolate, I would still trust in Thee, and still seek Thy kingdom; and if there were a possibility for me to be sent to hell, I would set UP FOR THEE there!" That was enough for the Devil; he went off, and has not troubled me since; and as we were singing—

"Jesus has satisfied,"

I said, "Yes, he does!" I have had many a hard battle, and been worsted many a time in learning this lesson of life—that God is THE GOOD OF HIS CREATURES. God is a jealous God. You know how you husbands would feel if you thought you had a rival in your wife's heart; or you wives, in your husband's; or you parents, in your children's. God is a jealous God, and he will be the first and last, and All and in All to the soul. He will have all creatures subordinate to Him, and used for, and in Him, and if you will do that, He will give you a happy time of it; but, if not, you will have a rough time of it. He *cannot* save you till you are brought to it, and if you won't make up your mind to it, you will be stripped and whipped again and again till you do, and if you will not, after all, you will be cast into hell. Now make your choice. I have made mine, and I will go through with it, and see how it ends. It has begun very nicely. I thought as I heard my third boy speak, "Yes! I would rather have him there than sitting on an emperor's throne, and swaying a sceptre over an empire."

Now, this is what God wants of every one of you. He says, "If you will choose Me, I will choose you. My eyes run to and fro over the whole earth, to show Myself strong on the behalf of those who will thus choose Me. If your heart is perfect towards

Me in this sense, I will put my great, long arm down, and I will hold you up and confound your enemies, vindicate your character, and bring out your righteousness as the sun. Trust Me, and I will look after you. I will choose your wife or your husband, if you are to have one, guide you and provide for you, be near you when sick, and with you when dying. Whether I allow your head to be cut off like John the Baptist's, or let you be martyred like Peter, never mind, I WILL BE WITH YOU, and you shall be WITH ME FOR EVER. Now, will you thus choose Me? Will you, will you?" The Lord help you, now and for ever. Amen.

The War Cry, No. 11.—March 6, 1880.

HOLINESS: YOUR REMEDY.

By the Rev. JAMES CAUGHEY.

Entire sanctification in an instantaneous salvation—that act of the Holy Ghost, according to our faith, by which sin is entirely expelled from the soul, when the blood of Jesus Christ cleanseth from all sin, and includes an instantaneous power then given, always to cleave to God. Thus, an excellent man remarked: It is gradual in preparation, but instantaneous in reception; and the more earnestly we long for this unspeakable blessing, the more swiftly the preparation increases. The gradual preparation is often short, when the soul wills it, earnestly desires it, quickly abandons all for it, and prays as it should.

A snake may cast its coat, but keeps its venom. A sinner may cast off much of the "old man" in outward and even in inward character, but if not cleansed from all sin, there is a snaky inclination in his nature that may wound others, or the cause of God, or himself eternally. That was a shrewd saying of one, that "a profession of religion without purity is like a fair glove drawn over a foul hand." Purity is the prime jewel of moral worth in man or woman. What is the most graceful dress humanity ever wore, if the one who wears it has a filthy person? We would shrink from such a creature; but such is he who makes a graceful profession of religion, and carries about him an unclean spirit, an impure heart; he lacks the prime jewel of moral worth—purity.

Let that new convert hearken! The remains of sin, yea, the seed of every sin is within till you are cleansed throughout spirit, soul, and body.

That was a good remark of one, "There is much of the old man in the new." Already have you been made sensible of the fact. Those seeds have taken root; they are rooted in that heart of yours, among the plants of grace, like weed-roots in a bed of vegetables. They must be uprooted, or they will destroy or dwarf the plants of grace within you. Indwelling sin is Satan's capital. He who has a small capital will keep adding to it. It is Satan's investment, and he will not neglect it; the Devil's stock, and he will watch its rise and fall in the market, close as any stock-jobber. Sin is in itself an accumulating principle. A slight cold is prone to additions. It is so with indwelling sin. Its nature is to render you cold to duty, and cold in your affections towards God and His people. It contracts the fine affections of your soul as a cold the fine vessels of your body, rendering you chilly and shivering in the presence of a good Gospel fire.

You have the elements of this ague within; it has begun, in fact, in these incipient stages. Get rid of it. The blood of Jesus Christ cleanseth from it. The medicine is ready if your faith is ready. Why not now? "All things are possible to him that believeth." May you have no rest till you are cured of these ague fits, slight, indeed, at present. It would be a wonder were it otherwise, considering your present advantages. But inbred sin has a lodgment in your nature, and every exposure to "evil air," to bad company, and bad influence will add to it. Your ague fits will increase.

PURITY OF HEART IS YOUR REMEDY. Be not deceived. Are you clear in your conversion? If not, in all liklihood you will wander back to the Devil.

Be not deceived in your intentions regarding sin. You have put it away, surely you have, if regenerated. But have you parted with it for ever, think you? Have you quite removed your eye off it? No treacherous inclinations towards it? No hankering after it? Do you hate it? There is much in that remark of one, "That many deal with their sins as the mother of Moses with her boy:" she put him away, but provided for him. Hid him in the ark of bulrushes, as if she had forsaken him quite; but kept her eye upon him, and at last became his nurse. Thus many leave but love their sins. They hide them from the eyes of others, but their hearts go after them. At last they take their sins to nurse and give them the breast. Can you detect anything of this in yourself? Then let me shout in your ears—"PERIL!" "Make a clean breast of it," as they say sometimes to criminals; resolve upon heart purity; it is your only safety. The blessing is your spiritual birthright if you are born from above. You will backslide, perhaps foully and fatally, without it.

Some years ago, a young lady in ——, since gone to heaven, lost her evidence of justification through some sore mental conflict or other; but one day, when listening to a sermon on Rom. viii. 16, she regained it. "Then," said she, "with the blessing of justification in one hand, I held forth the other for full salvation." That was the proper attitude for a truly justified soul. She soon after obtained the blessing. Can you separate green from a healthy and growing leaf and keep it healthy and growing? Or heat from fire and keep it fire? Or sunshine from the sun and keep it sunshine? As well try habitually to separate a desire for purity from your justification and keep it justification. God commands you to be holy—"Be ye holy, for I the Lord your God am holy." How can you continue justified in disobeying so plain a command? "For this is the will of God, even your sanctification." How can you retain the blessing in question with a will so contrary to God's will? You may answer these questions as best you can, they require none from me, only this: I would not like to trust the safety of my state to such a justification. It is deceptive and dangerous.

Holiness preserves itself and those who possess it; a high encouragement to seek it. Your not seeking it has been the CAUSE of your "sinning and repenting, and repenting and sinning again"—your constant oscillations between darkness and light, and light and darkness, aye, and of all your troubles.

The War Cry, No. 22.—May 22, 1880.

PURITY BY FAITH.

An Address delivered at the Holiness Meeting at Whitechapel, on Friday night, May 14th, 1880,

By THE GENERAL.

I AM announced to say a few words to-night on what is a favourite theme at these Friday night meetings, viz., Purity or Holiness by Faith. The Apostle Peter, in the 15th chapter of Acts and 9th verse, you will remember on the occasion of a very important convention or council of war, made the declaration that "God put no difference between the Jew and the Gentile." They wanted to make a distinction in the method of salvation between the one and the other. They wanted to get the Gentile to be saved in one way and the Jew to be saved in another way, and the Apostle came down with the positive affirmation, which I take to be an unalterable affirmation, that God puts no difference between one man and another—between Jew and Gentile—but that He purifies all hearts alike, purifying them by faith. In this early age of the Church there were as now perpetual bickerings and arguments as to that which constituted the nature of religion, and as to the methods by which the enjoyments and blessings and powers of religion were to be obtained. Men went on groping in darkness because they would not walk in the light. Some walked one way and some the other, the Holy Ghost at the same time indicating that there was only one common platform for all people and all nations, and that that platform was the one on which they should stand; and God, who is no respecter of persons, will not alter His plan to suit anybody. We, if we want this blessing, must go on this platform, and get it just in the same way by Faith.

There are persons here from different sections of The Army—different parts of London and the country, whose desire, I believe, is that there should be some definite teaching as to what is meant and what is taking place in these meetings, as to holiness of heart. God has put no difference between Jew and Gentile, or between one man and another, but, as I have said before, there is one common platform, one common salvation, and one common method He uses to purify their hearts by Faith.

We may here consider three or four points:—

I.—What God here proposes to deal with—the heart.

II.—What He proposes to do with the heart—to purify it.

III.—The nature and extent to which God does purify the heart.

IV.—The method by which this purity is obtained.

First.—WHAT GOD HERE PROPOSES TO DEAL WITH—THE HEART.

What does God want with me and from me? He has given Himself and His Son for me, and what more does He require from me?

He comes to me and says, "My son, give me thine heart." Now, when He asks for my heart I am not to understand that He wants this central source of physical power. He asks for that in the mind which answers to the heart in the body—the central controlling force, the great driving-wheel, the main-spring which determines the force and character of all conduct. It is this which he wants to control and direct. When, therefore, He comes and says, "My son, give me thine heart," and I give it to Him, He gets ME and everything I have, and He has a distinct right to all I have and all I am; and, my brothers and sisters, He alone can make this claim, and nobody is going to hold back that claim; we have the right to the privileges and blessings obtained by our obedience in giving God what He asks for; and now He says, I put in the claim for your hearts before you go any further, here, in Whitechapel. Hold! Stop! My son and my daughter, give me thy heart.

Second.—BUT WHAT DOES HE WANT TO DO WITH THE HEART IN THIS STATE?

This claim meets a man in the midst of sin and guilt. I suppose you know yourself better than anybody else, and I suppose if you could write down your own characters, some of you would give yourselves but a very sorry character at the best. Now has He some plan or scheme by which He can manage to get you through with this sin and poison in your soul, with this devilry and rottenness, and bitterness in your hearts, to get you through the gates? No; He wants to cleanse and purify you. His is not a scheme for covering up. He says to me, "William Booth, if you cover up your sin you shall not prosper; I am against it; I am not against YOU, but I am dead against your sin, and if you cover it up, or have any plan of hiding it from Me or the angels, and fancy you are coming out right, you shall not prosper, neither in this world or any other. That is contrary to the first principles of My government, and all my wisdom and all my power is against it; but if you will forsake sin it shall be well with you." We all know what some theology would do; how it would cover it up and tint it and gild it, still keeping the rottenness within. But this is not God's way. What does He want with my heart? He wants to purify it, and take the poison and corruption out of it, to take that out which, perhaps, has cursed my wife and children and neighbours, and is a curse wherever it goes; He wants to cast it out and destroy it.

Third.—TO WHAT EXTENT DOES GOD PROPOSE TO PURIFY MY HEART?

I am not going into any arguments as to what extent God can purify my heart here in this life. The general idea is that, in some form or other, some portion of sin is eradicated; and when we listen to some who tell their experience they indicate that there is a very considerable deliverance, that there is a very considerable difference between a saint and a sinner, and yet that there is some sin still in possession—a little, sometimes a great deal. You admit that the Lord can take away the sin, yet cannot admit that He can cleanse and purify every chamber of your soul. You say He has got the best sitting-room, always kept as nice as possible; and He has got the spare bedroom, which is always clean and sweet, and anyone is at liberty to walk in and see them; He has got the best rooms in your house, but that only makes Him a lodger after all! Don't you think you had better let Him have the whole house and you become the lodger? and then He will bear all the burdens of the rent, and the rates and the taxes. Everything made over to Him (cries of Amen! and a Voice: "Victualling and all!") and then you will have done with that miserable system of house-cleaning, which comes every now and then, when you have a revival and a great cleaning down, and turn the house out of the windows, and then go back and be as bad as ever.

Now the question is to what extent He is willing—to what extent He has promised—to what extent He has engaged—to what extent He leads me to expect He can and will purify my heart, and I answer in a word, A-L-L. "Then will I sprinkle clean water upon you and you shall be clean: from ALL your idols, and from all your filthiness will I cleanse you." There are hundreds of other texts which say and mean the same thing; and if the English language means anything at all, it means that His grace is sufficient. Sufficient for what? If it is not sufficient to make me the perfect master of the Devil; if not sufficient to keep me from the most abominable thing under the sun which God hates, and which crucified the King of Glory; if not sufficient to keep me from sin—His Grace cannot be sufficient for me at all. Some people go as far as to say it IS NOT. But I say, who told you so? I say, not only this Book says so, but my spiritual instincts confirm it. You never find a man getting on his knees and saying, "O Lord, save me from getting into a bad temper more than seven times a day!" "Give me, O Lord, the grace not to slander my neighbours above once a-week." You never say, "O Lord, I don't want to be carried away with the love of money so that I should not be willing to give anything at all!" But, rather, when you pray, you say, "O Lord, Thou dost deserve all my heart, here it is, take it, and purify it to Thyself." It seems to me that has been the proud boast of God's messengers for two thousand years all over the wide world that THE PLAISTER IS AS LARGE AS THE WOUND, that the remedy is equal to the disease. We know what sin is best when we know how God abominates it; that sin is the deadly Upas that poisoned His Son's life on Calvary. It is this sin that He wants to save us from, and if He wants to save me at all, He wants to save me now. I need go no further, and, if you will read your Bible, Jesus Christ's own declaration is, "Blessed are the pure in heart, for they shall see God."

Fourth.—HOW IS THIS PURITY TO BE OBTAINED? "Purifying their hearts by faith;" that is by faith instrumentally. It is God's own blessed, holy Spirit that purifies the heart. You cannot too clearly perceive this, that it is the Lord Himself who purifies, that we are to be purified according to His will—purified, bear in mind, not GLORIFIED, that is, not saved from temptation, not saved from sorrow, not saved from the possibility of falling again into sin. Salvation may be described as a book in three volumes: the book of Justification, which is a very nice volume to take in; the book of Sanctification, gilt-edged, and clasped; and the book of Glorification, which cannot be obtained down here. You can get the two first volumes now, and you had better have them both while you are about it—but you must get the other above.

God, then, engages to purify our hearts. God engages to do this Himself. You have not to struggle to purify and save yourself, but to bring yourself to God and trust Him to do it. There are several conditions in obtaining this blessing, and the one condition seems to me to embrace and include the other. If a man repents rightly, he believes rightly; and if he believes rightly, he repents rightly; and sometimes repentance is made to be the condition, sometimes consecration is made the test, and sometimes faith the means of obtaining what is sought after: one condition implies the other. The soul that wants to be pure, so far as it can, purifies itself. If a man wants to be clean, he washes himself; if a man wants to be saved from sin, and is willing to put himself into God's hands entirely, he passes from sin. If he wants to walk with God, God gives him the power to walk in the light.

There are three unalterable conditions:

1 says, "I am willing to give up sin."

2 says, "O Lord, I give myself to Thee."

3 says, "O Lord, I believe the blood does

cleanse and purify from all sin. I trust Thee now. Here I am, all sin and weakness; I am willing, I can go so far as that; I am willing to be healed. You are the Physician and You must heal me?"

Very well. Whatsoever things ye desire when ye pray, believe that you RECEIVE them—not that you have received them, not that you shall receive. If you put a sovereign in my hand, I don't say I believe I have it, I know that it is there—I feel it. But if you tell me you will give me a sovereign, if I have any faith in your word, I believe it, I expect it, I rejoice in the expectation; but when it is given I feel it, I know it, and testify to the fact.

Do you say, O Lord, cleanse my heart? O Lord, I give myself, body, soul and spirit to Thee? I am willing to be a clean man; I am willing to have a clean life, clean friends, clean companionships, a clean walk and conversation; clean business and everything else. I consecrate and dedicate myself to Thee, to walk clean before Thee if it cost me my life; and, O Lord, as Thou hast engaged, as Thou hast given Thy blood to make and keep me clean when I trust Thee, I trust Thee to do this just at this moment; and God, who cannot lie, has spoken, and will perform it, and I am saved and purified through faith in His own Almighty power?

The War Cry, No. 41.—Oct. 2, 1880.

FAITH EXERCISED.

By BISHOP PECK.

You have now reached a point in which the question of faith is of the first importance. You have renounced all dependance upon self; all trust in the arm of flesh. You have seen one after another of your earthly supports fail; you dare not trust again anything less than infinite power. You would not recall one worldly dependance which you have renounced. To you there is now absolutely but one hope, one confidence left, and you need no other. "Behold the Lamb of God which taketh away the sin of the world." Pause humbly, before the Crucified. You have now but one absorbing desire—to be cleansed from all sin—to be fully prepared to glorify God, and enjoy Him for ever. See now, the blood of Jesus Christ, which cleanseth from all sin. How entirely efficacious,—how completely it meets the demands of the Law,—how fully it pays your debt,—how sovereign the remedy. Dare you trust it? Nay, dare you do otherwise? You do trust it now;—you depend upon it for pardon, for acceptance, why not for Salvation from all inward defilement?

You long for the fulness, "In him all fulness dwells." Gaze for awhile into that throbbing heart. For you it beats with infinite love. You cannot—do not doubt His love. He suffered for you. He grappled with death for you. He rose from the tomb leading captive your captivity. How kindly He bore with you in your rebellion! With what compassion He lifted you up, and embraced you when you came all guilty and trembling, and fell at His feet. How He blessed you—forgave all, made you His child, His heir to all His blood had purchased! Can you doubt?

Call some precious Scripture to your aid. This, for instance; "For we have not an High Priest that cannot be touched with the feeling of our infirmities, but was in all points tempted like as we are, yet without sin. Let us therefore come boldly unto the throne of grace, that we may obtain mercy and find grace to help in time of need." Touched with the feeling of our infirmities!" Is it possible? The sympathy of Jesus! A revealed, a glorious fact.

You are in a condition to need sympathy. How great your infirmities. How deeply you have felt them. How weak and erring at every step, and how fearful that you should sometime fall to rise no more. How many efforts have you made to do better, and failed! How often in the morning have you risen, and on your knees covenanted that every moment of the day should be the Lord's, but when the night has come with what regrets have you sought forgiveness for your unholy tempers, your unguarded levity, your worldly desires, your want of devotion, or your idleness in your Master's vineyard! How strangely feeble when you ought to be strong; how timid and doubting when you should have triumphed in the power of living faith. Yes, you need sympathy. There you lie at the foot of the Cross. What can you do?

Christ is qualified to sympathise with you. He is a man; He is your weeping, sympathising Brother; He is a tried man; He has passed through every fiery ordeal. Remember the mountain and the forty days. Remember Gethsemane, the Bar of Pilate, and Calvary. He is a triumphant man. "Yet without sin." What a volume of meaning — what a comprehensive theology in these few words! He encountered the foe, and He conquered—conquered for you. See Him on Tabor, with His garments white and glistening. See Him rising from the tomb; stand with him upon Olivet, and see Him ascending, for you "He ascended upon high, He led captivity captive and gave gifts unto men"—here is triumph —here is victory—victory for you.

Just in this hour of your extremity, the grace of full salvation is here at your command. Come, and come "boldly." This, you will say, is a strange liberty for a worm of earth. How can a poor sinner be bold in the presence of his righteous Judge—the Sovereign of the universe? Surely, not on his own account—not in view of anything he has ever been, or thought, or felt, or done. If to himself alone he must look, it is right that he should shrink with alarm at the idea of an approach to God. But see; it is because we have a sympathising High Priest that we are to come "*boldly*." The degree of your confidence in this approach is to be the measure of honour you will confer upon your sympathising Saviour. "Boldly," because He pleads, and weeps, and prays for you, "boldly" for you to come at His own command to ask the grace you need; "boldly," for He bends towards you, and stretches out His wounded hands to receive you; "boldly," for He cannot deny himself, He will, must redeem his rich and gracious promise, and "save to the uttermost." Oh, trembling spirit, take courage; be not afraid of Jesus; come near to Him; fall into His arms; press closely to His bosom, that you may feel the throbbings of His heart of love. Let Him wrap you in His crimson vest, and you shall feel, and say, "The blood of Jesus Christ cleanseth us"—CLEANSETH ME—"from all sin." Now let your fears depart; no more shrinking or hesitating. With humble simplicity, with faith that receives Christ for everything—your wisdom and righteousness—sanctification and redemption—claim the answer to your prayer, and claim it now, "Cleanse Thou me from secret faults." "Create in me a clean heart, oh, God." You are urging the prayer; hear what your Saviour says: "Whatsoever ye shall ask in my name, that will I do, that the Father may be glorified in the Son." Here let your humbled spirit rest, claim the full efficacy of the atonement, for yourself, without a doubt. Do you now really do this?

Faith in the possible is one thing; faith in the

probable another thing; faith in the morally certain, another; and faith in the actual, another. The soul, gasping for purity, cries out, "I believe He is able to cleanse me." This is faith in the possible. "I believe He is willing"—faith in the possible strengthened. "I believe He is able and willing to cleanse me now, just as I am"—faith in the probable. "*I believe He will do it*"—faith in the morally certain. The last earthly reliance is renounced. "I BELIEVE HE DOES SAVE ME; I sink into His arms; the promise is sure, the renovating power runs through—the Spirit itself beareth witness; I believe that I receive the things I ask; I am saved — COMPLETELY, PERFECTLY SAVED;" this is faith in the actual. There are many witnesses to the truth of this description.

The War Cry, No. 31.—July 24, 1880.

WHAT MUST I DO?

NOTES OF AN ADDRESS

By W. BRAMWELL BOOTH.

HOLINESS, or wholeness, is looked upon by many as a state of grace greatly to be desired, by many as possible to attain, by many as a standing duty which they fail to come up to, who are therefore brought into constant condemnation. I think, my friends, that the case of such is perhaps more to be pitied, even if more to be blamed, than that of any other class of religious people. They are enslaved within the reach of liberty, they hunger within full view of the heavenly table.

Now, I shall take for granted that you are in the main agreed with me as to what is Entire Sanctification. Let me run through its main characteristics. 1. It is a distinct state of grace from justification. 2. It includes deliverance from all outward and indwelling sin, from unbelief, from the very *roots*—pride, anger, love of the world, &c. 3. It includes the filling of the heart with all the graces and fruits of the Spirit. The being perfected in love. Filled to present capacity, and kept filled as the vessel enlarges. Now, I say that I am taking for granted you go with me thus far, and I have said that you believe this possible, and that some of you are brought into condemnation every time you think about it, because it is not your experience. And this morning I am taking the question you will find in the 30th verse of the 16th chapter of Acts, "What must I do to be saved?" as a text on which to ground some remarks in answer to this question, What must I do to be sanctified? I believe there are many saints who could well ask, "What must I do to be saved?" and when you begin to do this, when you come to this matter with an earnest, longing, determined *heart*, you are not far from this *inner* kingdom of the kingdom of God.

I. WHAT YOU MUST NOT DO TO BE SANCTIFIED.

It seems to be important to point out one or two things which must not be done. So much has been said and written, and it is so easy to be *befogged*, especially when the Devil is ever on the watch to confuse.

1. *You must not think you have nothing to do.* That you have only to sit still and go quietly on, and that by some means God will work this change in you by growth. That you will grow out of these hindrances, that you will grow the better of that pride, and that evil temper, and that unbelief. This is a delusion. Oh, but you say, Am I not to grow in grace? Yes; but not *into* it. Take that apple-tree and plant it in the stony road, and bid it

grow *into* the orchard, and it will droop, and droop and die; put it in the orchard, and bid it grow *in* the good soil there, and it *will*, and fructify. Just so your *soul*. Get *in* this grace of entire sanctification, and then *grow*. Oh, what a delusion this is, "I am just to wait for God." It makes backsliders. What is the first cause of all backsliding? HEART EVILS! I know a gentleman who was asked—"Sir, how long have you been thus waiting and growing?" "Fifty years!" "And are you yet sanctified?" "No!" And yet he believed he would have been ten times more useful and happy if he had. He is, I believe, fully saved now. How do you think he regards that fifty years of doing nothing? I tell you, I regard it as *lost*.

2. *You must not say or think you cannot do what God requires you to do.* Here is a very subtle and fatal temptation of the Devil. He actually persuades some of you to think you *cannot* do what God requires. Beware of this. Satan lays before you the circumstances. Your home, your business, some idol, some one thing which you feel you cannot renounce. My friend, it is a *lie*. You feel this. This is hindering you. He is a liar. Oh, the sorrow, the bitterness, the failure, the condemnation we should avoid, if we did but thoroughly, clearly settle that he is, and always has been, and always will be a *liar*. The very fact that the Spirit of God calls upon you to do anything is proof that He is able to cause you to do it.

3. *Do not seek any easier way than God's.* The very essence of sin is selfishness; the very essence of Holiness is self-sacrifice. This is to be a life of

self-surrender, of self-nothingness, of utter carelessness and fearlessness about self. You are to *lose yourself in God.* Here is to be a new Almighty power in the universe—God the Father, and God the Son, and God the Holy Ghost, and you a godly being—four in one, and one in four. Abandon your poor, puny, miserable, greedy, self-seeking, self-indulging self. Away with it! Lord, away with him! Crucify him! Amen, and amen, and amen.

4. *Do not hold to anything doubtful.* I beseech of you be careful here. *Doubtful.* Anything about which you have a shadow of doubt. Because if it is in any degree doubtful it cannot be of *faith;* can it? Those two cannot go together; and "whatsoever is not of faith is SIN." Do you now see why you must give up that doubtful *practice*, that doubtful *habit*, that doubtful ornament you wear, that doubtful book you read, that doubtful companion you have? My brother, my sister, I tell you, in the name of the eternal God, it is SIN; and you must not hold to it. How I am struck with this. A dear woman, who was seeking this blessing, and wore a white rose in her bonnet, said to me, there was *no harm* in it. I asked, "Is there any good in it?" and then it was torn out, and the Rose of Sharon came into her heart. I don't say that in itself it was wrong; I don't deny I did think the bonnet looked a great deal more genteel without it; I only say it was doubtful; and to her it was sin, and it had to come out. I knew a man who treasured in his heart an undue affection for another, which chafed and marred his life; it got

there, and it would remain and did remain. It was a sort of bitter indulgence. It was natural—in its proper place, noble; but it had more place than its due, and it became doubtful. Before that man could be sanctified it had to be torn down. I have heard him say that the cutting down of that doubtful thing was the bitterest moment of his life, but that bitter stroke brought streams of preciously sweet and living water to his longing soul.

5. *Do not put the matter off.* This morning is the only time you can have in eternity as yours. Act in it. You have put off being holy long enough; too long. What is the regret of dying saints? "Oh, that I had been sanctified before." Payson said he had three months' experience of Heaven, and he might have had thirty years! That his ups and downs were his only regret there on his death bed. You will never have a more convenient season; you will never have *so* convenient a season. Thank God, all things are *now* ready. All remains with you.

6. *Do not despair about keeping the blessing.* You do not do this in other things. Your situation—you take one and lose it because of a failure or a fire. You do not go to the Union and say, "It's no use;" you laugh at the firm, and go and get another place; and you would be very much astonished if I came along and said, "Oh! don't do that; of course it would be nice to be in a good job, and have plenty to eat and drink, and something for the cause of God at Whitechapel, but really I fear you won't keep it!" Now, this is precisely what the Devil says. It would be nice to

have the grapes, and honey, and milk, it *would*, but you see you won't keep it! *A Liar.* A LIAR. Get your head up, and your heart; never despair.

II. WHAT YOU MUST DO TO BE SANCTIFIED.

Of course I can only give you the main lines on which the Holy Ghost operates. He will teach you, and, perhaps I ought to remark, that the first step is to lay your heart open to be taught what to do, and to be taught by God in His own way and now.

1. *You must understand what you have to do.* A mistake here is a vital matter. Here is a man in ill health; he is not laid up, but he is ailing. You say that man's first work should be to find out what is the matter, and to find out what to do to get well; you say he should not neglect it; you say he should at once get advice and medicine, and get to know how to treat himself. He may not understand *how* the medicine will cure him, but he may and must understand how to use it, and what to do. This is precisely your case; you must understand what to do. You may not be able exactly to tell wherein you are ailing or how this Balm of Gilead is going to effect a cure, but you must understand on what conditions, and how to apply it. So be at trouble to find out.

2. *You must be resolved to be sanctified at all costs.* You must be determined that as this is *God's* will, *you* will will it also, no matter what comes. This is essential. A feeble resolve will tremble and turn coward the very moment God puts the knife in. Let me suppose this man in ill-health is suffering from a tumour; the doctors say they can cut it

out and he can be well; he makes a sort of resolve, but, when he sees the knife, runs away. Now this won't do. Will you be holy? Learn then at once to resolve at all hazards that you *will*, and that you will not shrink when God's knife comes to cut out and cut off what is spoiling your spiritual health.

3. *You must forsake all, consecrate yourself and your all to and for God.* There must be absolute and total surrender of everything. Now, by this I do not mean that you are no longer to mix with your friends, or eat and drink, and conduct your business, but that you should cease entirely doing these for *yourself*—selfishly. You are called upon to hand over your all to God, to become His, and henceforth to act as His steward in the matter. Now bring them up this morning—family, friends, time, talent, business, money, reputation, all, all, ABSOLUTELY ALL. There now, lay them out at Jesus' feet, henceforth to be HIS and *not* YOURS. Do you? He will take them and take *you*. He will speak with those lips, and run with those feet, and gaze through those eyes, and work with that brain. *I declare them all to be His own; I proclaim Him Lord of all*, OWNER OF ALL, DIRECTOR OF ALL, LORD OF ALL. *Surrender!*

4. *You must believe that He does now sanctify you wholly.* "Believe on the Lord Jesus Christ, and thou shalt be saved." In this Bible we have no promise without its conditional *Faith*. Justification by Faith, Regeneration by Faith, Sanctification by Faith, Glorification by Faith. All else is but the ladder up to this final round, which shall lead you into the kingdom. Believe (1) that He is able and

willing to do this; (2) that He is able and willing to do it now, not to-morrow; (3) that if you now have faith He will now do it; (4) put your reliance or trust in Him now, believing that He *doth now do it*. Not has done, but that He now *doeth it*. Cast yourself into the arms of Omnipotent Love *now*. *Throw yourself down*. Take a leap, and do it now.

In conclusion, let me say this is a plain matter-of-fact question of *obedience*. God the father says, "Be ye holy." Christ says, "Be ye therefore perfect, even as your Father which is in Heaven is perfect." The Holy Ghost, by Paul, says, "Without Holiness no man shall see the Lord;" and, "therefore, leaving the principles of the doctrine of Christ, let us go on unto Perfection." *You must obey*.

I demand your decision. Be ye holy, and be ye holy NOW.

The War Cry, No. 18.—APRIL 21, 1880.

THE EXPERIENCE

OF

MRS. AMANDA SMITH.

MRS. AMANDA SMITH, a negress, with whose name our readers are acquainted, told her thrilling story with the strange weird pathos which long years of oppression have wrought into the negro's voice, yet with the dignity of a king's daughter, and with the simplicity of a little child:—

I was very definitely converted to God in 1856. I was very ignorant, but I had been taught that God would save me the moment I believed. I lived in the country in a family of "Friends," and went to town only once a fortnight. When I was convicted of sin I prayed, fasted, wept, read my Bible, but the more I read the more confused I got. I used to think my one trouble was disobedience, and it seemed to me I needed some one who had not sinned to intercede with Jesus for me. Therefore I cried to the wind, the sun, the moon and stars to carry my sorrow to the Lord: "O wind! you never sinned like me? tell Jesus I'm a poor sinner." When the sun got up and lighted the world I said: "O sun! you never sinned like me? tell Jesus I'm a poor sinner." At night, when the moon and stars were shining, I cried in my distress, "O moon and stars! you've never sinned like me, but kept your place as God has made you; tell Jesus I'm a poor sinner." Thus I pleaded second-handedly with Jesus through the Heavenly bodies; but, oh! the wonderful forbearance of God! I can't understand it.

I sat down one day almost in despair. The suggestion came—"You've been sincere; you've fasted, wept, prayed, read your Bible. You've been three months like this. God does His work quick: if He'd meant to convert you He'd have done it long ago. Give it up!" But it seemed as if the Holy Spirit said, "Pray once more." "Yes," I said, "and I'll be converted this afternoon, if there's any such thing as conversion." It was March 17, a bright and beautiful day. I got all my work as forward as I could, and then went down into the cellar and began to pray, "O Lord, convert my soul." The suggestion followed, "That's just what you've said many times before. It's no use." I began again, "O Lord, please convert my soul. If you'll only do it, I'll love and obey you all my life: O Lord, if not, I've come down here to die. Salvation or death! I'll never leave this cellar alive unless I have that which I've been praying for so long." Well, I did die; but I came to life again very quick. I said, "O Lord, I WILL BELIEVE." The darkness that had filled my heart so long all passed as before the noon-day sun. When I got a glimpse of Christ, my Saviour, my bonds were loosed, and I cried, "Why, Lord, I do believe; this is just what I have been asking for. O Lord, I do believe!" and down it came like a wave all through me again and again.

Why didn't they tell me it was like this? Why didn't they tell me it was only by believing God? I was a new creature. I was all new—my flesh, my head, my whole being. I rubbed my hands together and said, "Oh! I'm new!" You know what colour they are; but there seemed a halo over them. I made but two springs out of the cellar. The glory of God filled my heart. I wanted to tell someone, and I thought, Must I wait a fortnight before I can tell out my joy! How many times I had prayed for hours in that kitchen after they had all gone to bed? Now I struck the table at which I had so often knelt, and cried, "I'M SAVED!" and the table seemed to bound with delight. I wanted to see if I was the same. I might have been as green as grass or as black as the ace of spades, but I felt new. There was a large mirror in the parlour, and I went in there to see if I was the same, or if some wonderful change had come upon me.

When I told about it, some of my people said, "There'll be a vaccillation. Wait till the Devil fires a few bomb-shells, and you won't be as happy as you are now." Not being taught that God would sanctify and keep me, I was sometimes on the mountain, sometimes in the valley; but in reading my Bible and praying very much, I began to see that God had more of the same kind to follow, and being so much more it really was better than the beginning.

I had now begun to seek entire sanctification. I asked an elder what was meant by being "pure in heart." "O child," he said, "that means you must come as near to it as you can." I went home, but oh, this hunger and thirst after righteousness was not satisfied. When I was convicted for holiness I was in a clearly justified state. I had no doubt about my acceptance with God. When I was converted it was conviction of guilt; now it was conviction of want. As the hart panteth after the water-brooks, so my soul panted after God, the living God. "That comes to me what I want," I said, "it's God!" The elder said, "You must come to it as near as you can. What is the use of fretting yourself. Do all you can. Visit the sick, sing, pray!" But the hunger went on, and when I read, "Rejoice when men persecute you," I felt that was not my experience: there was a feeling of retaliation. And when they spoke about me and blamed me, I wanted to justify myself instead of leaving it all with God.

Then I read, "This is the will of God, even your sanctification." I went to the old deacon and asked, "What's the meaning of this?" "Oh," he said, "that's the blessing people get just before they die." Well, I didn't want to die; I wanted to live and work for God; and when they told me, "You'll never live this life till you die," I wanted to live and not to die.

In 1868 it pleased God to let me hear a sermon from Rev. J. S. Inskip, from the words, "Put on the new man, which after God is created in righteousness and true holiness" (Eph. iv. 23, 24). I had never read a book, or tract, or definite testimony, but now as the preacher went on, I followed like a child with its hand in its father's, and as he made point after point, I said, "Yes, that's plain." But I thought, if I got it, how shall I keep it? I didn't remember it was Christ keeping me. Mr. Inskip said, "When you are tired and go to bed, you don't think of asking how you're to breathe? and so if you get God dwelling in you, He'll live Himself in you." "Yes," I said, "I see it." Just then a mighty baptism—I don't know what else to call it—came down on me. Every nerve in body, soul and spirit seemed to feel it. A joy and power swelled up in my heart to overflowing.

The next point was that this blessing was instantaneously received, but the development would be continuous. "How long is a dark room dark after you take a light into it?" "Yes, Lord, I see it," I said, and down came this wonderful inexpressible something, bringing every thought into captivity to the obedience of Christ. The preacher went on: "If Jesus is able, in the twinkling of an eye, to change this vile body and make it like unto His own glorious body, how long does it take Him to sanctify a soul?" Quicker than the sparks fly from the steel I touched God, God touched me. Hallelujah!

The first result was the establishment of my faith in all God said. I believed all the Bible. At Keswick, last year, I looked out on that great mountain Skiddaw; a few weeks ago I saw it again. We have had a hard winter, but the mountain is not changed. I said, "O Lord make me like Skiddaw." The storms were real that beat upon Skiddaw, and it has been so in my experience—real fights and real difficulties. I don't see any apologies in the Bible for speaking about what the Lord has done for our souls. Oh, its God's. Glory to His name. The half has not been told.

"Of peace I only knew the name,
Nor found my soul its rest,
Until the sweet-voiced angel came
To sooth my weary breast,
The half was never told,
The half was never told,
Of peace divine so wonderful,
The half was never told.

The War Cry, No. 30. July 17, 1880.

THE SOUL AT REST.

THE sinful man has no true peace, because, among other sources of disquiet, his position is at variance with Providence.

One view to be taken of sin is, that it is war. It is not only war against God's character, but against His commands; not only war against His commands, but against His providential arrangements. God has one way and plan of arrangement; the sinful man, who is in a state of rebellion against God, has another plan. The centre of God's arrangements is benevolence, or the love of all; the centre of the sinful man's arrangements is the inordinate love of himself. Radiating from such different centres, the plans which are formed continually come in conflict. Under such circumstances it is impossible that the sinner should have rest. Finding himself face to face in opposition to what God has determined, and thus in conflicting lines of movement, he is continually met and counteracted, continually smitten and driven back. His life is a warfare commenced and carried on, and under the most hopeless circumstances; a warfare attended everywhere and unceasingly with discomfiture and suffering.

2. On the contrary, the man who is united with God in the possession of a common central feeling, is necessarily united with Him in all the movements and arrangements which He makes. In other words, he rests from the perplexities and uncertainties of making his own choice, which his Heavenly Father has made for him. With the exception of sin, God's choice never varies, and never can vary, from the fact and incidents of that state of things which now exist. And it is this choice, however painful it may be in some of its personal relations, which the godly man takes and sanctions as his own. So that his choice being already made by the unvarying adoption of that which is from God, he may be said not to have any preference of his own, but to rest from his own choice, that he may repose in God's choice. And God's choice is only another name for His providence. There is, therefore, no conflict; there never can be any.

3. God's providence extends both to things and events. Inanimate nature, even in the lowest forms, is under the Divine care. Not a rock is placed without a hand that placed it; not a tree grows without a Divine vitality, which is the inspiration of its growth; not a wave of the ocean rolls without the power of God's presence to protect it. The storms and the earthquakes are the Lord's. God is thus the life of nature. And the man who is in harmony with God has no controversy with

Him in any of these things. On the contrary, he accepts all, is at peace with all.

4. God is also the life of events, including in that term human actions. There is no good action which is not from God. The wisdom of the Supreme is the good man's inspiration. And, on the other hand, there is no evil action which God does not notice, and over which He has not some degree of control. The essence of evil actions, it is well understood, is the *evil motive from which they proceed*—a motive which is not, and cannot be, from God; but still, God will not allow the action, which proceeds from the motive, to take effect, except as He shall see fit. In other words, God has the prerogative, which can pertain only to an *infinite* being, of overruling evil, and of bringing good out of it. So that there is a providence of evil as well as a providence of good. And hence, the good man can be in peace even when the evil man triumphs, because he knows that the "triumphing of the wicked is short."

5. Again: God's providence is *internal*, as well as external. It is the inspirer of the feelings of the heart, as well as the director and controller of outward events. Our thoughts and feelings are from God, so far as they are right thoughts and right feelings. Accordingly, the man who is fully united with God, rests from all anxiety in relation to the particular form or feeling of his inward experience. Among the various thoughts and feelings which are right and good he has no choice. For instance, he does not desire inward joys, nor great illuminations of mind, nor freedom and gifts

of utterance; but desires and accepts only that degree of light and joy, whether more or less, which God sees fit to send. It is true we are directed to "covet the best gifts" (1 *Cor.* xii. 31), but it is equally true that those gifts are the best *which God selects and gives.*

In everything, in gifts and the exercise of gifts, for time and for eternity, the wise man chooses for himself what God chooses for him; which is the same as to say that he rests from choice, or that he is without choice. God's providence is his guide.

6. Rest, or pacification in God's providence, implies and secures the fact of rest or peace in other things which have an indirect relation to His providences. For instance, he who is at rest with Providence has rest *from vain and wandering imaginations.* He is unlike other persons in this respect, who constantly recur in their imaginations to other scenes and other situations, and people them with the felicity which is the creation of their own minds. If his imagination ever goes beyond the sphere which providence has assigned him, it does so under a Divine guidance, and not at the instigation of unholy discontent.

7. Again: he who is at peace with Providence, experiences, as one of the incidental results of his position in this respect, a peace or rest *from feelings of envy.* The occasion of envy is the existence, or supposed existence, of superiority in others. It is impossible, therefore, for him to envy others, because, viewing all things as he does in the light of God, he does not and cannot believe that the situation of others is better than his own, accord-

ingly, he is at rest from the agitations of this baneful passion.

8. He has rest also from *easily offended and revengeful feelings.* If he has been injured by another, he knows that his Heavenly Father, without originating the holy impulse, has seen fit, for wise reasons, to allow its application against himself. He receives the blow with a quiet spirit, as one which is calculated to strengthen his own piety, while he has pity for him who inflicts it. Considered in relation to himself, he accepts all, approves all, rejoices in all.

9. In the remarkable language of the Apostle Paul, which precisely describes his situation, he "Suffers long and is kind; he envies not; is not easily provoked; thinketh no evil; rejoiceth not in iniquity, but rejoiceth in the truth; beareth all things, hopeth all things, endureth all things."

The War Cry, No. 84.—July 28, 1881.

IN THE HEAVENLIES.

By DANIEL STEELE, D.D.

FOLLOWING the custom of tourists in foreign lands, I give you a description of the country in which I have happily sojourned nearly five years. I must confess that I have more than a traveller's interest in this land, since I have become a naturalized citizen, and settled down in it for life.

This country was named by one Paul, a daring explorer, who flourished at the beginning of the Christian era, and who, like the writer, became so enamoured of its charms, that he ever made it his permanent abode. It so closely resembled Heaven that he took that term and transformed it into an adjective noun, "The Heavenlies," and wrote it down on his chart as the new country. This new name he uses five times in his report to the Ephesians, and nowhere else.

Some recent travellers who have not diligently studied Paul's chart, either driven by severe storms from the ordinary track of voyagers, or, more likely still, through the guidance of Paul's pilot, whom he took on board in Damascus, have found this earthly paradise, and, assuming the right of original discoverers, they have christened it "The Higher Life." This new name, though rather confusing to the novice, has not altered the thing. "The rose would smell as sweet under any other name." This Rose of Sharon, this isle of verdure and orange blossoms, fills with fragrance all the air for leagues and leagues around.

My great surprise, after entering this Eden, and feasting on its sweetness, was at the sparseness of its population. For the land is exceedingly broad and fruitful, capable of sustaining, with its abundance all the millions who are moistening the unwilling earth with their sweat, and compelling it to yield them a scanty sustenance. Why do they not migrate to these salubrious climes? This question I have been pondering over ever since I drove my tent stakes into the mellow soil of these flowery plains. At last I think that I have got at the truth of the matter. The false report has been industriously circulated through all the world that Paul's discovery was an optical illusion, a mirage in the distance, with bubbling fountains, shady trees, rich vineyards, and olive-clad uplands, all painted with fiery fingers on the clouds through a peculiar state of the tropical atmosphere.

Now, it so happens that the real-estate owner, or "ruler of the darkness of this world," who boasts, with too much truth, that he possesses all the kingdoms of this world and their glory, keeps this falsehood going with a very lively step round and round the world, lest the truth should be believed and leave his estates a habitation of bats and a "place of dragons." This wily despot dislikes to see his dominions depopulated to colonize Paul's "Heavenlies," and so he is ever busy denying that any such place exists on the face of the whole earth. Now it is nothing wonderful that this theory almost universally prevails to-day, since the aforesaid world-ruler has actually succeeded in accomplishing so adroit an act as to get thousands of Paul's successors solemnly to aver that they have diligently sought for "The Heavenlies" in all latitudes and longitudes, and to publish as God's truth that no such place exists under the heavens. The lie, which millions believe of their own accord, myriads will surely believe if it falls from the lips of their religious teachers.

Another reason for the sparse population is that, of the few who do believe that this land is a reality and no myth, a large number are deterred from entering by reason of the narrow channel through which they must force their way, and they are afraid that, in entering "The Heavenlies," they will loose too much of their idolized earthly. This narrow pass is The Way of Holiness. Hear Paul,—"Blessed be the God and Father of our Lord Jesus Christ, who hath blessed us with all spiritual blessings in The Heavenlies in Christ . . . that we should be holy, and without blame before Him in love." Holiness is the only gate into this blessed region, which many are afraid to enter.

But you are hungering for a description of the country itself. As its name indicates, "The Heavenlies," includes Heaven. The glorified Jesus is said, in chap. i., 20, to be at the right hand of God in "The Heavenlies," "in human form, locally existent." In chap. iii., 10, "principalities and powers," or spiritual intelligence of a higher order, are located in "The Heavenlies." But in chap. i, 3, Paul and the Ephesian believers are represented as "in The Heavenlies," and in chap. ii, 6, they are sitting "together in The Heavenlies in Christ Jesus," the "sitting" implying permanence of abode. This phrase, then, must include more than the Heaven which centres in the radiant person of Jesus. Heaven laps over upon the earth. A segment of earth has been annexed to Heaven. In my youthful days, before I had looked into international law, I one day asked Father Taylor, of the Seamen's Bethel, where in the Atlantic was the boundary within which the child is born an American citizen. His weather-beaten face lighted up with a smile that rippled from the centre to the circumference, as he replied, "My boy, there is no such line in the mid-ocean; we own clear across."

Locate Heaven wherever you please, it stretches clear across these earthly shores, and even takes in a slice, which Paul calls "The Heavenlies;" King James' version, "heavenly places;" and Bishop Ellicott, "the heavenly regions." This is nothing less than a high and serene Christian experience, in which the gracious Jesus manifests Himself to the spiritual eye of the perfect believer, and he enjoys constant communion with the glorified Head of the Church through the Holy Spirit, which makes him "a habitation of God."

The War Cry, No. 38.—SEPT. 11, 1880

SEVEN SANCTIFIED SOULS.

THE following brief extracts from the testimonies of eminently holy and eminently useful servants of God are to the point:—

Rev. John Fletcher.—"I will confess Him to all the world; and I declare unto you, in the presence of God, the holy Trinity, I am now 'dead unto sin.' I do not say, 'I am crucified with Christ,' because some of our well-meaning brethren say, 'By this can only be meant a gradual dying;' but I profess unto you, I am dead unto sin, and alive unto God. He is my Prophet, Priest, and King; my indwelling holiness; my all in all."

Rev. William Bramwell.—"The Lord, for whom I had waited, came suddenly to the temple of my heart, and I had an immediate evidence that this was the blessing I had been for some time seeking. My soul was all wonder, love, and praise. It is now about twenty-six years ago; I have walked in this liberty ever since. Glory be to God! I have been kept by his power. By faith I stand. . . . I then declared to the people what God had done for my soul; and I have done so on every proper occasion since that time, believing it to be a duty incumbent upon me. For God does not impart blessings to his children to be concealed in their own bosoms."

Rev. James B. Taylor.—"I am ready to testify to the world that the Lord has blessed my soul beyond my highest expectations. People may call this blessing by what name they please—'Faith of Assurance,' 'Holiness,' 'Perfect Love,' 'Sanctification.' It makes no difference with me whether they give it a name or no name; it contains a blessed reality, and thanks to my Heavenly Father, it is my privilege to enjoy it: it is yours also, and the privilege of all, to enjoy the same, and to go beyond anything that I have ever yet experienced. . . . . . Some, I expect, are a little disaffected to think I profess the doctrine of Perfect Love. They do not understand, because they have not experienced it."

William Carvosso.—"Just at that moment a heavenly influence filled the room; and no sooner had I uttered or spoken the words from my heart, 'I shall have the blessing now,' than refining fire went through my heart, illuminating my soul, scattered its life through every part, and sanctified the whole.' I then received the full witness of the Spirit THAT THE BLOOD OF JESUS HAD CLEANSED ME FROM ALL SIN. I cried out, 'This is what I wanted. I have now got a new heart.' I was emptied of self and sin, and filled with God."

Dr. Adam Clark.—This great and good man sought and obtained a clean heart in the twenty-second year of his life, and writes as follows to Mr. Wesley:—"I regarded nothing, not even life itself, in comparison of having my heart cleansed from all sin; and began to seek it with full purpose of heart. Thus I continued looking for it, and frequently in great distress, till December, 1782, when I opened my mind to a local preacher, who, I had heard, was a partaker of this precious privilege; from him I received some encouragement and direction, and so set out afresh in quest of it, endeavouring, with all my strength, to believe in the ability and willingness of my God to accomplish the great work. Soon after this, while earnestly wrestling with the Lord in prayer, and endeavouring self-desperately to believe, I found the change wrought in my soul, which I endeavoured, through grace, to maintain amid the grievous temptations and accusations of the subtle foe."

In after life Dr. Clarke said, "It has been no small mercy to me that, in the course of my religious life, I have met with many persons who professed that the blood of Christ had saved them from all sin, and whose profession was maintained by an immaculate life."

Bishop Hamline.—He says, "All at once he felt as though a hand, not feeble, but omnipotent, not of wrath, but of love, were laid on his brow. He felt it not only outwardly, but inwardly. It seemed to press upon his whole body, and to diffuse all through and through it a holy, sin-consuming energy. As it passed downward, his heart as well as his head was conscious of the presence of this soul-consuming energy, under the influences of which he fell to the floor, and, in the joyful surprise of the moment, cried out in a loud voice. . . . . For a few minutes, the deep of God's love swallowed him up; all its waves and billows rolled over him."

Mrs. Hester Ann Rogers.—"I was deeply penetrated with his presence, and stood as if unable to move, and was insensible to all around me. While thus lost in communion with my Saviour, He spake these words to my heart: 'All that I have is thine. I am Jesus in whom dwells all the fulness of the Godhead bodily. I am thine. My Spirit is thine. My Father is thine. They love thee as I love thee. The whole Deity is thine. He even now overshadows thee. He now covers thee with a cloud of his presence.' All this was so realized to my soul, in a manner I cannot explain, that I sunk down motionless, being unable to sustain the weight of His glorious presence and fulness of love."

The War Cry, No. 74.—May 19, 1881.

CONSECRATION.

By THE GENERAL.

Can you illustrate the kind of Consecration God wants, before He will sanctify me throughout, body, soul and spirit?

A long time back, in this country, there was a war between the king and the parliament, and the greater part of the nation took the side of the parliament, and the king was sorely pressed. It was then no uncommon thing for a nobleman or rich person to come into the king, and say, "I am sorry and ashamed that your majesty should be driven from your throne, and be suffering all this indignity and disgrace, and I want to help your majesty to get your rights again; and I have come with my sons and my servants to place our swords and our lives at your disposal. I have also mortgaged my estate and sold my plate, and brought the proceeds to help your majesty to carry on the war." Now, *that* was *a real consecration* to *that* king: *it was the laying of life and substance at his feet.*

Now, that is just the kind of consecration God

wants—only, one that goes deeper down still. He has been driven from His throne in the hearts of men everywhere. His name is cast out as evil, and men universally refuse to have Him to reign over them. Now, Jesus Christ wants to secure the kingdom for His Father, and appeals for true-hearted soldiers who will help Him to succeed in this great undertaking, and He wants you to come into the camp in the *same spirit* that these men of old did to their earthly king when he was in those desperate straits—to come, saying, "I bring my goods, my influence, my reputation, my family, aye, my life. I will have no separate interests: use all I have and am to promote the war, so that my King shall have His own, and His throne shall be established." That is consecration in reality, and *that only*. This is what Jesus Christ taught when He said, "Seek first the Kingdom of God." This is what Jesus Christ exemplified in His life and death. This is what Paul and the first Apostles did; and, if you are to be a thorough Christian, you must be consecrated in the same way.

Then a true Consecration has in it the nature of a Sacrifice?

Decidedly so. It is *a real sacrifice.* It is the presentation or giving away of all we have to God; a ceasing any longer to own anything which we have hitherto called our own, but all going over into God's hands for Him to order and arrange, and our taking simply the place of servants, to receive back again just what He chooses. This, it will be perceived, if a reality is no *easy* task, and can only be done in the might of the Holy Ghost; but, when it is done, when all is laid on the altar—body, soul, spirit, goods, reputation, *all*, *all*, *all*—then the fire descends, and burns up all the dross and defilement, and fills the souls with burning zeal, and love, and power.

"Wherefore, seeing we also are compassed about with so great a cloud of witnesses, let us lay aside every weight, and the sin which doth so easily beset *us*, and let us run with patience the race that is set before us."—*Hebrews* xii. 1.

Is not true Consecration something in common with CRUCIFIXION?

Yes, undoubtedly, it is a real crucifixion. Crucifixion was an ignominious, painful death; and consecration means dying to all those pleasures and gratifications which flow from the undue *love of self*, the *admiration of the world*, the *ownership of goods*, the *inordinate love of kindred* and *friends*, which go together to make up the life and joy of the natural man. To do this is always a painful task, and yet we *must* be *crucified with Christ if we are to live with Him*.

"I am crucified with Christ; nevertheless I live; yet not I, but Christ liveth in me: and the life which I now live in the flesh I live by the Faith of the Son of God, who loved me, and gave Himself for me."—*Galatians* ii. 20.

You say Crucifixion is IGNOMINIOUS *and* PAINFUL?

Yes! but the pain is transient, and generally swallowed up by Divine joy. Afterwards comes the joy of being able to suffer and endure for Him in whom the soul delights. And this love—the bond of perfectness—so overtops the love of other things, and the pain of suffering and deprivation, that one is able to glory in the cross on which the crucifixion took place.

"But we glory in tribulations also: knowing that tribulation worketh patience;

"And patience, experience; and experience, hope."—*Romans* v. 3, 4.

Is it possible to rise above ignominy as well as pain?

Certainly. If a man is dead to the praise of the world, if he, like God, counts the wisdom of the world to be foolishness—if the change has really been wrought—represented by the word *death*—so long as he remains thus changed—thus dead—he despises the shame.

"Who for the joy that was set before Him endured the Cross, despising the shame."—*Hebrews* xii. 2.

Is not a complete consecration of the utmost importance when seeking Holiness?

Undoubtedly. Without a real consecration there can be no true Holiness. And it is generally on account of defective consecration that some souls experience so much difficulty in the exercise of faith for purity. There cannot be *full salvation* without *full surrender*. God can neither save nor keep what is not given to Him.

"Yea, doubtless, I count all things *but* loss for the excellency of the knowledge of Christ Jesus my Lord; for whom I have suffered the loss of all things, and do count them *but* dung, that I may win Christ."—*Philippians* iii. 8.

The War Cry, No. 91.—Sept. 15, 1881.

EFFECTS OF SANCTIFICATION.

By THE REV. J. A. WOOD.

Some of the precious results of the cleansing power of Jesus in my soul have been,—

1. A sacred nearness to God my Saviour. The distance between God and my soul has appeared annihilated, and the glory and presence of divinity have often appeared like a flood of sunlight, surrounding, penetrating, and pervading my whole being. Glory be to God, that even the most unworthy may be brought nigh by the blood of Christ.

2. A sense of indescribable sweetness in Christ. The fact that He is "The Rose of Sharon," "The Lily of the Valley," "The brightness of His (the Father's) glory," and "Is altogether lovely," has at times so penetrated my soul, as to thrill and fill it with ecstatic rapture. O how glorious and lovely has the dear Saviour appeared to my soul, and how strong the attraction of my heart has felt towards Him! Often His glory has shone upon my soul without a cloud.

3. A deep, realizing sense of the reality of spiritual things. Bible truth has appeared as

transformed into reality. The doctrines of the Gospel have become to me tangible facts, and my soul has triumphed in them as an eternal verity.

4. A surprising richness and fulness of meaning in the Scriptures, which I had not before realized. Many portions of the word, which I had hitherto but little understood and taken but little interest in, now appeared full of meaning, and exceedingly precious to my soul. The following passages have been applied many times to my soul with great power: "And I will pray the Father, and He shall give you another Comforter, that he may abide with you for ever: even the Spirit of Truth, whom the world cannot receive because it seeth Him not, neither knoweth Him; but ye shall know Him; for He dwelleth with you, and shall be in you.

"If a man love me, he will keep My words; and my Father will love him, and we will come unto him, and make our abode with him." "Now ye are clean through the word which I have spoken unto you. Abide in Me, and I in you. As the branch cannot bear fruit of itself, except it abide in the vine, no more can ye except ye abide in Me." "But if we walk in the light, as He is in the light, we have fellowship one with another, and the blood of Jesus Christ His Son cleanseth us from all sin." "God is love, and he that dwelleth in love dwelleth in God, and God in him. Herein is our love made perfect, that we may have boldness in the day of judgment; because as He is, so are we in this world. There is no fear in love; but perfect love casteth out fear, because fear hath torment. He that feareth is not made perfect in love."

5. A complete satisfaction and resting in Christ. Since then, there has been no favourable response from within to temptations from without. Before, I often found elements in my heart siding with the tempter, and felt that all was not right within. There appeared to be an aching void, or a place in my soul which grace had never reached.

But since Jesus sent the refining fire through and through my poor heart, I have been sweetly assured that grace has permeated every faculty and fibre of my being, and scattered light, love, and saving power through every part. Hallelujah to Jesus! I have found satisfaction, rest, and exultation in Christ.

6. A great increase in Spiritual power. This I have realised in my closet devotions, in my pastoral duties, and especially in the ministrations of the blessed truth. Blessed be the Lord, I have learned by experience that men may receive the Holy Ghost in measure limited only by their capacity to receive and feeble ability to endure. God could easily bless men beyond the power of the body to endure and live, if He were disposed to take them to Heaven in that way.

This increase of power has delivered me from all slavish fear of man or of future evil. It has given me such a love to the Saviour and to His glorious Gospel, as to make all my duties sweet and delightful. Truly, "Her ways are ways of pleasantness, and all her paths are peace."

7. A clear and distinct witness of purity through the blood of Jesus. The testimony of the Holy Spirit, and of my own spirit, to the entire sanctifi-

cation of my soul have been more clear and convincing than any I ever had of my regeneration, although I had no doubts of that for years before the Lord extirpated inbred sin from my soul. "Meridian evidence puts doubt to flight."

Dear reader, how I wish I could tell you how clear and sweet the light of purity has shone through the very depths of my soul! How I wish I could tell you the complete satisfaction I have realized since I obtained this pearl of great price! If I could only tell you all about the full and perfect love of Christ! But, oh! It can never be told! Its fulness, its richness, and its sweetness can never be expressed! You can know it only by experience, and this is your solemn duty and most exalted privilege. Will you not seek it? Will you not begin now? A holy life is the happiest life, the easiest life, and the safest life you can live. O, be persuaded to settle the matter at once, and begin now to seek for purity, and never yield the struggle until you obtain the glorious victory!

I might have written much more in regard to my weakness, unworthiness, and imperfections, and would have done so had I supposed it would honour Christ more than to write about the fulness of His grace and the riches of his love.

My experience is not my own, and it is in the hope that my humble testimony to the fulness and freeness of the grace bestowed upon me, the most unworthy, may encourage and lead others to avail themselves of this fullness of Christ, that I record my experience of the perfect love of Christ. I have given but a brief and imperfect sketch, a mere outline of the mercies that the Lord has heaped upon his poor servant. To him be all the glory.

Dear reader, seek holiness. At all hazards seek it. Expect no rest until your soul is made "free indeed" in the blood of Jesus. And when once you have tasted the blessedness of purity, you will never be able to be sufficiently thankful that you were induced to seek it. If you do not seek it, the period is not distant when you will never be able to forgive yourself for the neglect.

And now, reader, "I commend you to God, and to the word of His grace, which is able to build you up, and give you an inheritance among all them which are sanctified."

The War Cry, No. 62.—FEB. 24, 1881.

OBEDIENCE TO THE LIGHT.

AN ADDRESS AT THE HOLINESS COUNCIL, ST. JAMES'S HALL, FEB. 5, 1881.

BY MRS. BOOTH.

"I beseech you, therefore, brethren, by the mercies of God, that ye present your bodies a living sacrifice, holy, acceptable unto God, *which is* your reasonable service.

"And be not conformed to this world: but be ye transformed by the renewing of your mind that ye may prove what *is* that good, and acceptable, and perfect will of God." —*Romans* xii. 1, 2.

I HAVE been thinking about the word in the text, "*that*"—"That ye may prove what *is* that good, and acceptable, and perfect will of God." This advance in the Divine life, as well as every other, right to the end, till we advance into glory, has its *conditions*. The conditions of the advance from an absolutely unawakened worldly condition, to that of a convinced sinner, IS THE RECEPTION OF THE LIGHT. God awakens and enlightens thousands, and tens of thousands reject the light, instantly put it away, shut their eyes, will not have the light; these go back into greater darkness, and sin with more alacrity than ever they did before. Those who receive light, become convinced of sin—awakened, enlightened souls.

The next condition of advance from the state of a converted, struggling sinner, willing to part with his sins and to follow Christ *is faith* ; to believe in the Lord Jesus Christ, that he may receive the forgiveness of sins. And every advance onwards, if the believer is ever to get beyond the first principles if he is ever to grow a single inch, so to speak, there is a condition involved in that advance! For instance, if after conversion, the Holy Spirit reveals to him something which is inconsistent, which he did not before see, the condition of his advance another step is the *renunciation* of that thing! The reception of the light, and OBEDIENCE TO IT—and if he shrinks from, and does not receive and obey the light, he will never advance *any more* until he does. There are thousands of Christians instead of advancing have gone back since their conversion, because they would not comply with the condition "that they might prove the good and acceptable and perfect will of God."

There was a condition. They would have proved it, if there had been no condition; but there was a condition they would not comply with. They would not receive and obey the light. So there they stick, just where they were; or, rather, they have gone back.

Well, now then, here is a condition to *this* grand and glorious advance from the state of justification —where, while the believer is given power over sin, so that it does not rule over him, yet he sometimes, through its inward workings, falls under its power—the advance from this comparatively sinning and repenting condition on to that platform where the soul so abides in Christ that it sins not, that it loves God with all its heart and soul, and mind and strength—so united to Christ that walking in the power of the Holy Ghost, it fulfils the law of love under which it is placed, the advance, I say, from that up and down, in and out, falling and rising state, to this higher platform, also has its *conditions*.

You would go up to it to-day if it were not for the conditions; most of you would go up in a body as the Israelites would have gone into Canaan, if there had been no condition. I never knew any one so foolish as not to want to be in the good land; they want to be in, of course, and they would go in and get the honey and the milk, but there are the CONDITIONS! Now, then, here you have it plain, and you have it in numbers of other passages equally plain.

There is nothing upon which the Holy Ghost has been more particular than in laying down the conditions. And what are they? "And I beseech you, therefore, brethren, by the mercies of God, that ye present your bodies a living sacrifice." The living man—all of you; not IT, something in you.

That term is never used by the Holy Ghost when speaking to Christians, but *you* yourselves, *ye*, *you*, *your* bodies, *your* souls, *your* mind, the whole man —YOU—"a living sacrifice, holy, acceptable unto God, which is your reasonable service." And is it not? Is it too much? Is it more than He bargained for when He bought you? Is it more than He paid for? Is it your reasonable service.

And now, then, comes the conditions: "And be NOT CONFORMED TO THIS WORLD, BUT BE YE TRANSFORMED by the renewing of your mind, THAT ye may prove."

Oh, if you could be transformed to Him and conformed to this world at the same time, all the difficulty would be over. I know plenty of people who would be transformed directly, but to be not conformed to this world, how they stand and wince at that! They cannot have it at that price. As dear Finney once said, "My brother, if you want to find God, you will not find Him up there amongst all the starch and flattery of Hell. You will have to come down for Him." That is it, "Be not conformed to this world."

Nothing wounds me more, after being at meetings for dealing with souls, where I have tried to speak in a most pointed and thorough way to make everybody know what I meant, when I go to the dinner or supper table, people have not known a bit, or if they have, they won't accept it. Oh, this is the secret—they will not come down from their pride and high mightiness. But God will not be revealed to such souls, though they cry and pray themselves to skeletons, and go mourning all their days. They will not fulfil the condition—"Be not conformed to this world." They will not forego their conformity even to the extent of a dinner party. A great many that I know will not forego their conformity to the shape of their head dress. They won't forego their conformity to the extent of visiting and receiving visits from ungodly, worldly, hollow, and superficial people. They will not forego their conformity to the tune of having their domestic arrangements upset—no, not if the salvation of their children and servants and friends depends upon it. The *sine qua non* is their own comfort, and then take what you can get, on God's side. "We *must* have this and we *must* have the other, and then if the Lord Jesus Christ will come in at the tail end and sanctify it all, we shall be very much obliged to Him; but we are not going to forego these things."

Oh, friends, friends! I tell you this will never do. God helping me, I will, I must tell you, because it is driven in upon my soul by what I am seeing and hearing every day. People come to these meetings, and they groan and cry, and come to us for help, and we exhaust our poor brains and bodies in talking to them and giving them advice, telling them what to do, and when it comes to the point we find, "Oh, no, don't you be mistaken; we are not going to sacrifice these things. We cannot have the Lord, if He won't come into our temples and take them as He finds them. We could not forego these things."

You remember the text that was read at the opening of the meeting, "and the world hath hated them because they are not of the world, even as I am not of the world." It means something, and there are a hundred other texts teaching the same truth. NOW WHAT DOES IT MEAN? The Lord help us to see it. Does it not mean that we are not to be like the rest of the world? That we are not to be guided by the same measures and act upon the same principles as the world—that we are not to attach the same importance to mere earthly and worldly things that worldly people do? Have you ever thought of those awful words in the parable of the sower. "The desire of other things enter in and CHOKE the seed," not abominable things, not immoral things, not shameful things, but the *desire of* other things. And, in another text: "*Who* MIND *earthly things.*" They attach more importance to worldly things, and other things, than they do to the things of His kingdom. They practically make these things FIRST, though they sing about His kingdom and profess to make Him first; they make the earthly things first, and therefore they will not have their earthly things upset for His things, and do you suppose He is cheated? Do you suppose He is deceived? Do you think it is likely that the great God of Heaven, who has millions of angels and archangels to worship and serve Him, is going to pour His glory on such people, and reveal Himself to them, and use them? Not likely! "I will be first in your love," He says.

You women here, if you knew that you were not the first and only one in the affections of your husband, what would you say? And you husbands, would you dwell with a wife if you knew you were not the only one in her affections, but that they were divided between you and some one else? "Not likely!" you would say; "I am not going to lavish my affections, and my society, and my gifts, and everything I possess, on one whose heart is divided with another." "If she will have her heart divided, then she must go to that other."

Now, you know God is a jealous God, and He

knows who do mock Him, and He knows who will not sacrifice this conformity to the world, that they may walk with Him in white; and He knows who do not care what anybody thinks of them, or what people say of them, who are willing to be counted fools and fanatics that they may walk with Him and promote the interests of His kingdom, and who only regard their bodies as His instrument and their homes as His temple, so that their breakfast hours, or dinner hours, or luncheon hours, or any other hours, may be upset, and, in fact, everything made subservient to the interests of His kingdom. We must place everything at His service—our children, business, homes, and everything. If I understand it, that is nonconformity to the world.

Before we close, let me say a word to try to help those who are desiring to attain this blessing. There is no other way. It is of no use beating about the bush. Be not conformed, but be ye transformed. These two are in juxtaposition. If you will be conformed then you cannot be transformed; if you will not be conformed, then you shall be transformed. Now will you give up conformity to the world? If so, you may, every one of you be transformed this morning—go up into the land. You may all be saved to-day, and make your abiding place in Christ, and have all the power and glory which come to them that possess Him; you may advance from the miserable condition of a poor up-and-down, in-and-out wretched man, on to the glorious vantage ground of a saved man and a saved woman. The Lord help you. Amen.

The War Cry, No. 103.—Dec. 8, 1881

SUGGESTIONS TO OPPOSERS.

By W. BRAMWELL BOOTH.

I.

THERE are some things worth remembering in considering the opposition always offered with more or less violence to faithful and definite teaching and testimony on Holiness. Especially are they worth remembering by the opposers themselves, and to them I commend the following simple suggestions as worthy of some thought, with the assurance of my love in the Lord to all who may read these lines :—

1. Well then, to begin with, it is no proof against the doctrine of Perfect Love, it is no strengthening of any case which is made out against it, it is no help in the search for what is true concerning it, *to call it bad names*. It is at least a cowardly, and insincere, and hypocritical opposition to this teaching to misrepresent what is put forward as an authentic statement of doctrine, or a correct standard of experience. There is absolutely nothing gained to the cause of truth in

the earth by calling hard names, and abusing what is found difficult to refute. When we are accused of teaching "Sinless Perfection," we remember quite well, that, over and over again, this charge has been denied, nor can there be any proof given in support of it, from either the writings or teachings of any who have enjoyed the experience of a clean heart, or taught its attainability. We do not claim it. To say we do is to make a pretence, which we know full well *is* a pretence, and those who make it must know it too.

2. It is not wise to repeatedly assert as fact, that which all those who in every age, and of every church, have received this gift of purity, are agreed in declaring to be contrary to their experience. *We do not claim any ground of boasting before God.* We do not set ourselves up as being anything in ourselves, rather are we awake now as never before to our own emptiness, and nothingness; to our own utter unworthiness. But on the other hand, the soul that has received the Sanctifier in truth, can, does, *must* boast in HIM, must magnify His saving grace, and speak out and say, that once a bondman, slave, he is now come into the promised land, and dwells there, and eating of the fruits while walking in the liberty thereof, doth no longer want, and doth no longer doubt, doth no longer fear, doth no longer seek his own, *doth no longer continue in sin*, doth find ALL-CONQUERING, CLEANSING, KEEPING, GRACE abound continually, abundantly, EXCEEDING ABUNDANTLY, above all he can ask or think. Surely this boasting IN THE LORD, doth glorify Him, and Him alone. Doth sanctify

His name among the heathen. *The humble shall hear of this and be glad.*

3. The heart which has renounced the world, the flesh, and the devil, and which has, by divine grace, renounced its own, henceforth, to seek the things that are Jesus Christ's, is found with all its powers, ranged on the side of right and truth, on God's side. Full of Divine love, it loves what God loves, wholly, and hates what God hates, wholly. Hence, to maintain the experience of entire harmony with God's will, it is an absolute necessity, and never-failing condition *that we rebuke sin, and expose and denounce error wherever we find it.* It must be. God cannot be divided against Himself. God will have us declare openly, in spite of a universe in rebellion against Him, *to be against rebellion.* To say so, to make men's lives a misery to them because they sin. It will appear, to them and others, uncharitable; it will appear as though we had no sympathy with all that *is* good or godly in them. It will create misunderstanding, mistrust, divisions, and separations. *It will cost us a great deal,* as it did Moses, and Jeremiah, and Daniel, and Jesus Christ, *but it must be.* He who walks in the light as HE is in the light, and has fellowship with Him can have no fellowship with darkness, or the fruits thereof, can only have hatred and loathing for it, can only have rebuke or warning, in love, for those who love it, because their deeds, or some of their deeds, are *evil.*

To the wholly sanctified child of God, there is needed *a daily baptism of love,* to do this work, and to do it well. A daily mellowing down into tenderness and compassion, that the unflinching thrust of the Spirit's sword may be done without hurt to the thruster, and with quickly following balm to the wounded soul. *But it must be done.*

4.—It is an easy thing to announce that those who teach Salvation from sin "*lower the standard,*" that their witness to the presence and power of Jesus, as a Saviour of His people from their sins, is rendered of no value because of "wrong ideas of sin," and "low ideas of God's requirements." But what are God's requirements? what does the moral law demand of us all, and what does God's Gospel of Grace propose to enable us to be and to do in regard to it? That we LOVE. That "love out of a pure heart" be the motive power, the main spring, the guiding end of all our life, and all our desires, and all our deeds. That we love THE LORD OUR GOD with all our heart, and mind, and soul, and strength, and our NEIGHBOUR as ourselves. This *is* the standard. Nothing less, nothing more than this.

Ah, it is not we who have lowered it, but rather those whose words so plainly suggest that God will not regard in wrath those of His own who fail to fully obey His Word, that He will wink at their shortcomings, and count them without condemnation, because they have a standing in Christ Jesus; though, sometimes, they do walk after the flesh, and, sometimes, do fulfil the lusts thereof. *This*, indeed, is lowering both the standard and the Saviour; is making Christ the minister of the sin which He came to destroy, and degrading in the presence of a mocking world the eternal purpose of the True One, that where sin abounded, grace should much more abound.

No, no! we will keep the standard up. A life of love. A life of liberty. A life of victory. Of purity. peace, and power. This God requires, and requiring this, offers you grace to *raise you to it*, Remember *that*. Anxiety about the demands of God's law should not make you forget or underestimate the abounding provisions of God's grace, leaping to meet you at every point of weakness, and failure, and nothingness. Remember His riches as well as your need.

The War Cry, No. 104.—DEC. 15, 1881.

SUGGESTIONS TO OPPOSERS.

BY W. BRAMWELL BOOTH.

II.

LAST week, I remarked that there are some things specially worth remembering by those who oppose faithful and definite teaching, and testimony on Holiness, and I add to what I then wrote the following simple suggestions as worthy of some thought, with the assurance of my love in the Lord, and my earnest desire that God, the Holy Ghost, may lead every reader of these words into "the fulness of the blessings of the Gospel.'

5.—We are not unfrequently charged with *failing to give due reverence to the Bible as the Word of God.* If it is meant that we attach more importance to the *Spirit* than to the *letter*, that we have discovered after a practical experimental fashion, that the letter *killeth*, but the Spirit giveth *life*—we admit that to be so—but the holy soul can admit no more; to him, the Word of Truth is the meat and drink through which he receives the sustenance of his very life. He eats it. It is the chart by which the

Captain of our Salvation directs his every movement. It is the weapon with which, by the indwelling power of the Holy One, he is able to smite his foes, and overcome the King's enemies. He loves it. Illuminated by the Holy Ghost, he finds it yields him a new revelation of the Divine Will every time he looks into its pages. By it he tries the spirits around him. By it he tries himself.

Beloved, you who walk in the Light, remember that the Light cannot be darkness. He cannot contradict Himself. His Spirit in you will be in harmony with His Word, even when He speaks to your inward consciousness apart from the direct words of the Bible, which, if you know anything of communion with Him, He will.

To extol the PROMISER, surely cannot be said to take honour from His *promise*. To wait on the Lord for continual guidance, to trust in Him for continual cleansing, to rely wholly upon Him for continual keeping. To do this, puts upon His Holy law and precious promises the highest honour He has asked for them. This we will do. This we do. In return, He doth write His words upon our hearts, and engraves upon them "His new, best name of love." The LIVING WORD is with us.

6.—"Know ye not that your bodies are the Temples of the Holy Ghost." It is required that the body be the *willing and obedient servant* of a sanctified will and a holy heart. In itself the *instrument* either of sin or righteousness, it is to be yielded freely to obedient service, kept under, governed, by the power of a Divine indwelling, fulfilling in peace all the holy will of God, towards Him, and towards its neighbour. A means of glorifying God. A weapon of war to resist the Devil. A dwelling-place for the Most High. A workshop filled with powers, He himself created, and then redeemed, and now will sanctify, for God to work in for His own glory.

7.—It is a serious mistake, a mistake which may have eternally serious consequences, to measure one's own responsibility by another's, or to reckon another's attainments by one's own. Equally is it a terrible error *to regard the standard of one's present experience as the ultimate end of God's will concerning us.* If you are a doubting Christian, your own consciousness bears you witness that you are; but do not look upon that witness as evidence that there is nothing better than doubting for you, or for your brother. God's Spirit will testify to what you are, not to what you are not: to what you are, not to what you ought to be. Some people seem to rest because they *are* condemned, because they *are* cold, because they *are* unbelieving, because their hearts *do* deceive them, and accept that evidence as a token of peace instead of a sounding alarm of danger, and urgent entreaty to go on and know something better of the Divine will. To many it is a glorious fact, indisputable, ungainsayable by Satan himself, that God the Holy Ghost will as surely bear witness that we love Him wholly, with all our heart, as that we love Him much, but not Him alone. If you, a justified soul, *know* you are pardoned, you have living evidence that God can reveal His mind, and have the strongest cause to believe that your brother who declares the fact, *knows* he is sanctified wholly and saved from sin.

8.—That *we do not rejoice in the resurrection, power, and glory of a risen Jesus*, is a singularly strange mistake. To us He is risen, indeed. Captivity is led captive. We have good reason, some of us, to remember the days we spent at Calvary. The pardon by a dying Saviour, the cleansing which came by an open fountain of water and blood, the reconciliation of the Cross, these we well remember. Days of joy and peace they brought, but not days of *complete liberty*. We found not always power to rejoice, power to believe, power to obey, power to die. We needed a Jesus in resurrection power, and we know, who have a clean heart, when He came, how He came. We know He raised us to sit with Him in heavenly places, to have conversation above with Him, riches above in Him, glory above by Him, and, from that hour, His presence in us, and His pleading presence at the Father's right hand have secured us all our strength, and supplied us all our need. We loved Him on the Cross, and embraced Him in the tomb ; but, risen, He is with us, "the living," risen to rule and reign over us who are risen with Him, never to die any more. Blessed be this first-born of many brethren, the First-Born FROM THE DEAD.

The War Cry, No. 13.—March 20, 1880.

REV. W. FLETCHER'S TESTIMONY.

"My dear brethren and sisters, God is here! I feel Him in this place. But I am ashamed; I would hide my face in the dust. I have dishonoured my God and denied my Saviour, by not confessing Him. I have grieved His Spirit, I have been ashamed and afraid to declare what He hath done for my soul; but I am sensible of my folly, and deeply humbled on account thereof, and He has restored my soul.

"Last Wednesday evening, He instructed and commanded me by His word, 'Reckon yourself, therefore, to be dead indeed unto sin, but alive unto God, through Jesus Christ.' I obeyed the voice of God, and now obey it, by declaring to the praise of His love, I am freed from sin; yea, I now bear witness to the glory of His grace; 'I am dead indeed unto sin, and alive unto God through Jesus Christ,' who is my Lord, and reigns over every motion of my soul.

"I have received this blessing four or five times before; but I grieved the Spirit of God by not making confession, and as often I let it go. I lost it by not observing and obeying the order of God, who hath told us "With the heart man believeth unto righteousness, and with the mouth confession is made unto salvation,' which latter I neglected. Once the tempter suggested, 'What you feel cannot be the blessing; perfection is something higher. You are not delivered from mistakes, ignorances, real errors in judgment, in memory, etc., etc.; therefore, though you are delivered from sinful tempers, you ought not to make a profession that you are holy.' I listened to these things, and soon discovered I had lost what God had bestowed.

"When I had re-obtained the same glorious deliverance, the bait was offered under another form. The enemy now said, 'Wait a few weeks or days, and see if the fruits of sanctification appear, before you profess so great a salvation!' I had no sooner yielded to wait for the fruits, but I began to doubt of the witness, which before I had felt in my heart; and was in a little time sensible I had lost both.

"A third time, with shame I confess it, I was kept from being a witness for my Lord by the suggestion, 'Thou art a public character, a city set upon a hill; the world and professors have all an eye upon thee; and if some future trial should overcome thee, or if, as before, thou shouldest by any means lose the blessing, what a dishonour and reproach will it be to the doctrine of heart holiness!'

"A fourth time Satan prevailed over a worm by, 'It is true, thou art now freed from sin,—thou knowest that Gospel perfection is perfect love; that love is the fulfilling of the law, not of Adam, but of Gospel grace; and that many ignorances, mistakes, etc., are consistent with perfect love; but how many thousands will not believe this! How many affirm that every transgression of the Adamic law—the law of perfect innocence suited to Adam's sinless nature. Every transgression of this law is sin! and, therefore, if thou profess thyself free from sin, all these will give thy profession the lie. Enjoy, therefore, what God hath wrought in thy soul, and hold it fast, without declaring publicly I am freed from sin; I am holy; I am perfect in love.' But again I found, 'He that hideth his Lord's talent, and improveth it not, from that unprofitable servant shall be taken away even that he hath.'

"Now, my friends, you see my folly. I have confessed it in your presence; and now I resolve in your presence also, henceforth I will confess my Master to all the world. And I declare unto you, in the presence of God, the Holy Trinity, I am now 'dead unto sin.' I do not say, I am crucified with Christ, because some of our well-meaning brethren say, by this is meant a gradual dying unto sin, for a man who is crucified is a long time in dying; but I profess unto you I am *dead* unto sin, and that as effectually as my original nature was free from righteousness. But then, if our good brethren will still insist every ignorance, every involuntary mistake is sin, we will not quarrel: then in this sense I am not freed from sin. But if I may venture to believe my Lord Jesus, if love be the fulfilling of the law, then I know these things are consistent with love, with a single eye, and a pure heart; and I therefore dare to reckon thus in the presence of you all; and I mean to declare myself henceforth, before men and angels, 'dead indeed unto sin, and alive unto God, through Jesus Christ.'

"Mind it is still *through* Jesus, and *in* Him; not independent of Him, or separate from Him. He is my indwelling holiness. He is my All in All. He is all I want, and I wait for the more full and entire fulfilment of that prayer of His, 'Let them be one in Us.' O for the fulness of the dispensation of the Holy Ghost! O, my brothers and sisters, pray, pray for the outpouring of the Spirit! Wrestle, agonise with God till it is given.

"And now, you who are hungering and thirsting after righteousness, what wait you for? Delay not, unite yourselves to Jesus, your Holiness, by believing; take to yourselves this great salvation; take it now. You must receive it by faith: faith lays hold and says, "It is mine." As when you reckon with your creditor, and when you have paid all, reckon yourself free, so now reckon with God. Jesus hath paid all for thee—purchased not only thy pardon, but thine inward holiness. Now it is God's *command*, 'Reckon thyself dead unto sin,' freed from sin, and alive unto God, now, this moment. O, reckon now! Fear not; believe, believe, believe! and continue to believe every moment; for it is retained as it is received, by faith alone. Whosoever thou art that wilt perseveringly believe, it will be as a fire in thy bosom, and constrain thee to confess with thy mouth the Lord Jesus, and in spreading the sacred flame of love, thou wilt be saved to the uttermost.'

After Mr. Fletcher had ceased to speak, about thirty rose and witnessed for Jesus, that they also, through grace, were dead to sin, and alive to God. Numbers were so affected that they could not speak. I felt what was truly unutterable; I sank into nothing, and was lost in the fulness of the Triune God.

The War Cry, No. 50.—Dec. 4, 1880.

REPROVE.

Address to Officers.

By COMMISSIONER RAILTON.

1. It is an almost unknown thing for the Lord's people to continue in the zeal of their first love. Almost all fall back, after a shorter or longer time, into a much colder state, and many become backsliders in heart. These things are fully dwelt upon in Mrs. Booth's "Practical Religion,"* and especially in the chapter on "Heart Backsliding."

2. In the army men are prevented from falling back so far as this, in many cases, but, nevertheless, remain in a very poor and uncertain state, daily sinning and repenting, loading themselves and others with sorrows by their want of consistency and devotion, yet daily being brought back to the Lord, and so kept from ruin.

3. Even among the best of this latter class, who,

* "Practical Religion," by Mrs. Booth, 1s.

by steady growth in grace, and by the pressure brought to bear upon them in Holiness meetings and in other ways, have been led to give up drink, tobacco, dress, and many other evil things. There is a great want of understanding as to the will and power of God; and many who really appear to enjoy a continual light, and to be themselves earnest and valuable lights in the world, remain, unsanctified, simply for want of proper teaching. Consequently, some extraordinary trial, such as a change of officers, or the evil speaking or ill treatment of a comrade, will throw them back into the reserve list.

4. Nothing is so great a hindrance to the sanctification of our people—many of whom are in the greatest earnest to be, and to get whatever God desires—as the mixture of false with true teaching, and there is no subject upon which there may be so much good talk, not absolutely false in itself, but none the less false in the impression it produces, leading people to believe they are all right, when they are just missing, perhaps, only by a very little, the mark of the prize of their high calling. Better ten thousand times ordinary soldiers of The Army, ignorant of the whole matter, than soldiers who imagine themselves sanctified, owing to some false teaching, when they are not.

5. Just as no one can be saved until they are penitent, so none can be sanctified until they are made truly penitent, on account of the evils of their own heart and of their doings, therefore, nothing so much tends to prevent anyone's being

made holy as the daubing of untempered mortar, the sweet and pleasant teaching and singing prevailing so largely to-day, and causing persons to enjoy delightful feelings of satisfaction, when God is not satisfied with them.

Continually press everyone as to whether they are perfectly satisfying God, and, as almost all are consciously grieving Him at times, trouble them about this and show how serious it is, and how fatal it may be, till they are made thoroughly wretched on the subject. Just according to the degree to which a man is made to feel himself wretched, whilst tied to sin and grieving God, will be the heartiness and thoroughness with which he will give himself up to be fully delivered, and will rejoice in perfect deliverance.

As your knowledge of men increases, you will be able to describe their feelings and inconsistencies, and shortcomings, so clearly, that they shall see the secrets of their hearts, set in the very light of God's face, till they are made to tremble in His presence. Incessantly repeat the changes in public and private, so that your very appearance shall remind your brother of his faults. Let all your life show the same light.

6. The great villainy of the day amongst God's people is the making void His law, the pretending that we who are saved are set free from any sort of binding obligation, and cannot be by any means condemned.

So much the more is it needful for us ceaselessly to press upon His people the law of God, which was made so much more binding by the priceless gift of His son to us, and is made so much more extreme in its requirements under the perfect illumination of the Holy Ghost. Do not allow any conscience to become easy whilst failing to pay to the very last tittle all that God now claims from us, and whoever is satisfied with less than this is a robber of God.

The 1st Epistle of John and the Revelation, which most clearly set forth what God wishes us to be, abound in the most violent expressions as to those who come short of His requirements in any way. The more perfectly you love God and men, the more earnestly and clearly will you protest against any wrong committed against Him, inwardly or outwardly.

Ceaselessly show how entirely we are required to give ourselves up to God and to be and do all that He desires, and especially dwell upon the ingratitude of any holding back from a neglect of Him who freely gave Himself up for us all.

The War Cry, No. 107.—Jan. 5, 1882.

PURIFY YOURSELF.

The GENERAL'S Address at Exeter Hall on Boxing Day, 1881.

The General,—I want to read you the three following verses, and to make a few observations on the last of the three:—

"Behold, what manner of love the Father hath bestowed upon us, that we should be called the sons of God: therefore the world knoweth us not, because it knew Him not."

It does not know that we are divine; it only knows us as the Salvation Army, or professors of religion. It does not know our divinity.

"Beloved, now are we the sons of God, and it doth not yet appear what we shall be: but we know that, when He shall appear, we shall be like Him; for we shall see Him as He is."

"And every man that hath this hope in Him purifieth himself, even as He is pure."

Every man and every woman that hath this hope in him or her, this hope of seeing Him in the glory, this hope of being with Him in the "Hallelujah Country," purifieth himself even as He is pure.

Now, let me talk to you Salvation Army people as though none of our brothers-in-law had come to see us.

I will suppose that some morning there comes to your door a carriage, and out of this carriage there jumps a man all dressed up in livery, with gold buttons, and lace, and I know not what. He asks if you live there and says, "I want to speak to the master and mistress—I have brought a letter." You open this letter and you find that it is an invitation from the Queen of England for you to go and take your children to spend a month with Her Majesty, at Osborne House, in the Isle of Wight. I think your first exclamation would be, "This must be all a mistake. This must be a hoax. The Queen knows nothing of us. Who are we that we should have this honour?" However, I will just suppose that you are satisfied that this is a real affair, and that you are to spend a month with Her Majesty. Suppose, also, that the letter intimated you were not to be troubled about the expense, that Her Majesty would see about your travelling, and take care of your affairs while you were away, and engage to be your friend, and the friend of your children after you return home.

Now, then, after the first flush of excitement has passed away, and you have written letters and told your uncles, and aunts, and cousins, and all your neighbours and friends, and the Captain of the Salvation Army, and assured him that, if the Queen does anything for you, the Army shall share your prosperity. I imagine, then, you settle down, and your wife would say, "Now, John, we must get ready for this visit," and after making inquiries as to how you were to behave yourselves, and what you were to say, and telling your children how they must bow and curtsey, and all sorts of things which are appropriate on such occasions, "Now," you would say, "what sort of clothes are we to appear in?" I fancy I can hear the woman saying, "Well, John, your coat is uncommonly poor: you have had it so many years, and since you have taken to wearing it all day Sunday, instead of letting it lie at your uncle's for three or four months of the year, it has worn down uncommonly fine, and as for your trousers, you wear them out a great deal at Knee-drill, so that they are hardly fit to be seen. However, I will tidy them up;" and I think I see the good woman as she nearly brushes away the bit of nap there is left. Then she says, "Anyhow, we will be clean before Her Majesty. We have not got much to set ourselves off in, *but we will be* CLEAN, and the poor woman gets the soap and the tub, and rubs the bits of things almost to pieces, and says, "I will make them as white as snow."

Now, my friends, no such invitation ever came to your house, nor is it likely that one should: but do you know this, that you have an invitation, all of you (for we are not bothered with any theology that shuts anybody out), not to go and spend a month with the Queen of England at Osborne House, but to spend an eternity with God in the High Royal Court of the King of kings.

I am sure that there is in every breast here, who

has the hope of one day standing in the presence of the Lord Himself, with all that august and royal gathering that will be there, the feeling that he must prepare himself, that he must make himself ready for the occasion, that he must

PURIFY HIMSELF.

Whatsoever other preparation you may feel necessary to make, there is an instinct in the breast of every real child of God that holiness is indispensable in order to see the Lord. That you must have a clean heart, and clean thoughts, and clean feelings—that you must purify yourself even as HE IS PURE—in order to stand before God, to be ready to spend your eternity with Him.

There is a question often asked in connection with this purifying—as to how far, and to what extent we can be purified down here, in this London, in this very place where I live—to what extent can I be delivered from evil, saved from sin, purified and prepared for the great gathering in that great Home of Heaven? It seems to me that this passage with the greatest clearness, and, to my heart, the greatest satisfaction, answers the question—"Every man that hath this hope in Him *purifieth himself.*" How far does he purify himself? "EVEN AS HE IS PURE."

Now, my comrades, there can be no controversy as to how far the Blessed Master is Holy, how far He is pure. It is a settled question with us all—our own instincts, apart from the Book of God, answers that question. He is Holy, and the Holy Spirit says here distinctly and definitely, and beyond all controversy, that "every man that hath this hope in Him, purifies himself even as He is pure." He makes himself in some way, which we will endeavour to show, clean—He so purifies himself that there is no sin left. It does not say he hopes, or seeks, or desires, or tries to purify himself, or that he hopes when he comes to the river of death he will, in some mysterious way, find himself purged from sin, or that he expects to pass through some kind of purgatory on the other side the river; but it says, in the present tense, that every man that hath this HOPE IN HIM, not the man who is in Heaven, but the man who is looking towards it and expecting to come to it, purifieth himself.

I am not talking about perfection now, I am talking of purity. Now purity is a very simple thing. If a vessel is clean, it is clean. If a garment is clean, it is clean. If a man's heart is clean, it is clean. Jesus Christ said, "Blessed are the pure in heart." He did not mean half pure, but hearts that were entirely pure. We are assured by the Holy Spirit, who never uses words without the corresponding meaning, that the blood of Jesus Christ cleanseth us from *all* sin. And the Holy Ghost says in various forms again and again, "Then will I sprinkle clean water upon you, and ye shall be clean." "Purifying their hearts by faith."

Now, what does it mean? Can it mean anything else but taking all the sin away? I don't want to quarrel with anybody as to the use of terms. Some people say, "I will go all the way with you till you come to talk about the roots. "*Come with me all the way, and say that the blood of Jesus Christ can cleanse from all sin.*" *But if you won't go with me all the way* I WILL LEAVE YOU BEHIND. I am going *all the way, all the way with the Bible, all the way with the cleansing blood,* all the *way with the power of the Holy Ghost.* I believe the plaister is as large as the wound, and I believe God Almighty has power to save men and women to the uttermost, that he has power to fulfil His promise and to supply ALL OUR NEED.

If we do not show you the way of full cleansing, go somewhere else and find out the way, and then come and tell us if you have found out a better way. But there must be some blessed balm that can perfectly cure the soul? Thank God, there is a Physician that can meet the case! He *healeth, cureth,* ALL *thy diseases.*

One of my children—and perhaps it may have been the same in your home—once on a time suffered from that deadly disease called small-pox. When the child was getting better, if the doctor had come, and said to me, "Well, Mr. Booth, I think we are getting on very nicely, very nicely indeed, for the child is almost well; I think nearly all the poison is out of it. I think now you should settle down, and be thankful without wanting a perfect cure. I do not think there is very much of the disease left." I should have turned round and said, "Doctor, you won't do for me, I will send for that other doctor round the corner. What are you?" "An Allopath." "Oh! then I will try the Homœopath, and if he won't do,

I will try the Hydropath; and if the Hydropath won't do, I will try all the other 'paths,' but I will have all the poison out. I want the child to be CURED. You said you could cure her. What is the use of telling me that you are going to leave a little poison in her." My brethren and comrades, some poison has got into the veins of my soul, and into yours, and into the veins of our children, and here is the Great Physician who comes down and says, He is ALMIGHTY TO SAVE. But you stand up, you ministers, and you deacons, and you professed followers of Him—you whose work it is to glorify and publish His fame, and look Him in the face, and me too, and say, "He is Almighty to save SO FAR, but there must be a little poison left." Oh! may God, I say, drive this God-dishonouring idea out—out of every heart. He is mighty to save, and that to the uttermost. Thank God, there is a way of purifying—there is a pool of Siloam—there is a balm in Gilead—there is virtue in the blood. The blood of Jesus can cleanse from all sin! And every man that hath this hope in him purifieth himself EVEN AS HE IS PURE.

"Well," you say, "Don't go any further. I believe every bit of it. But tell me HOW it is going to be done." "Every man that hath this hope PURIFIETH HIMSELF." Let me put out one hint here. I know many people who are very anxious to get their neighbours purified. They are very anxious that other people should be purified. I think it will be a very good thing if you just stop and purify YOURSELF first, and then go on with your neighbours. The Lord help you. How is this work going to be done? He purifies himself. I believe in human responsibility. Perhaps I go as far as most people in recognising human accountability—that we are accountable to God for our conduct here, and that we shall have to give an account of all the opportunities we enjoy of getting blessing, and of blessing other people. I believe thoroughly, therefore, in human responsibility; that a man makes his own bed before he has to lie on it, and there may be some here who are making a bed for themselves in Hell. Oh! the Lord turn you round, for that is a very bad business. You will have to make your bed in Heaven. In this sense I mean, that God puts within reach of every man the means and opportunity of perfecting his own purification. But you say, "How is this going to be effected?" Take the answer in other words of the Holy Ghost, spoken elsewhere—"Having these promises, dearly beloved, let us purify ourselves, cleanse ourselves, from all filthiness of the flesh and spirit, perfecting holiness in the fear of God." This passage follows on to the commandment, which says, "Come out from among them, and touch not the unclean thing, and I will receive you, and you shall be my sons and daughters." Having, therefore, dearly beloved, these promises of purification, let us, WITH THEM, cleanse ourselves, our thoughts, our feelings, our hearts, from all filthiness of the flesh, and of the spirit, perfecting holiness, not merely in the streets of the New Jerusalem, but down here in London, in the presence of the Lord.

Let me give another illustration. I will suppose

that there have been some very bad times in trade. You have been out of work fifteen or sixteen weeks. You have exhausted all your resources. You have pledged and sold all your available garments and goods, and you don't know what to do. There is no fire in the grate—no food in the cupboard, no credit at the shop. You don't know what to do. You sit with your head on your hand, and your wife walks aimlessly about the room, agonised to hear her children crying for the bread that she has not to give. I open the door and walk in; "What is the matter?" I say, "You seem to be in low water. I am a stranger to you, and you are a stranger to me, but I've heard of your distress." You tell me your story, and I say, "I can help you, and I will very gladly do so." And I put my hand in my pocket and pull out a piece of crumpled paper, open it and lay it out, and say, "This will relieve your present necessities. Go, and *with* it get some bread, and fire, and meat, and some boots and clothes to keep these poor little dears warm, and when you are warmed and fed, and made comfortable, come to me over the way, where I have a factory, and I will see if I can't find you something to do in the future." I disappear while your wife is pouring out her thanks, and you can't speak because a great lump comes up in your throat, and you don't know what to say even if you tried to, you were hoping that the "missus" would do it, because she does things of that sort so much better than you. At last, you come to yourself, and the first thing you do, I think, is to take out the banknote and look at it. It reads, "I promise on demand to pay so-and-so £5," and you look again, and see it is on the Bank of England. Now you say, "Here is food and fire, and all we want to satisfy all our present need." What do you do with it? Do you put it in the old teapot without a spout in the corner cupboard, and keep it as a great treasure, or do you take and pin it in the Family Bible, and bring it out and read it at family prayers morning and night, and say, "Oh! what a blessed promise I've got! What a wonderful promise this is! Oh! my dear children you must all be so happy now, and my dear wife you must not cry any more. I have this wonderful promise! What a dear good man he was to give me this promise." If you acted thus, your wife would say, "My dear, I'm afraid that trouble has touched your mind," and the children would say, "I can't see any good in that, father. I thought it was something that had to do WITH BREAD AND FIRE and a PIECE OF MEAT; what makes you say it is such a good thing." No, No, you say, "Come along Jack, bring the basket, tie a piece of string on for a handle, and then give me that bag, it will hold the bread," and away you go, and first of all you march off to a great big building, called the bank, open the folding doors, and walk up to the counter, and spread out the note on the counter, and the young man looks at it, and then at you, and then asks, "Will you have gold or silver?" "Aything you like, only let me have it." You take the money, and away you march to the butchers and bakers, and grocers, and that promise on that crumpled piece of paper, makes you downright happy. This man having the promise, what did he do with it? Why, with it he fed himself, his wife and his children, and made his wretched home into a little heaven below.

And now, my dearly beloved, having these promises of purity, promises of cleansing, promises of a full Salvation, promises of joy, promises of power, WHAT SHALL WE DO WITH THEM? I know what some of you have done with yours! You have been committing them to memory ever since you were a little child. You know them all by heart, and you read them in the morning and at night, and you compliment the Lord because of them; but there is nothing else. You say, "I want a clean heart. What is the promise for? What must I do with it?" *Go to the bank, and cash it, of course.* Go to the heavenly banker, and say, "Here, my Lord, here it is with your own signature attached to it, and sprinkled with the blood of your precious Son. Now, my Lord, come and fulfil it all in me. Amen. Oh! give me this cleansing. Come and purify my heart. I do believe, I will believe, that you will do, nay, that you do unto me, according to your own words." Go to the bank with it, and having these promises, dearly beloved, you shall be cleansed from all filthiness of the flesh and of the spirit, and every man that hath this hope in Him, he purifies himself, and has the witness in his own heart that he is purified, and having the fulfilment of the promise, he gives God all the glory of it. And being cleansed from pride, it doesn't make him proud; and having all the conceit taken out of him, it doesn't make him conceited; and being humbled at the footstool of Divine mercy, it doesn't exalt him. "He purifieth himself, even as He is pure."

My brethren, put away all the difficulties which Satan and unbelieving people have put into your hearts. Come in all the simplicity with which this man would go, under the circumstances I have described, to the bank, and present that promise, and receive the cash, so do you come to the Great Banker of the universe with His own word. It is either His word, or it is not His word. He either promises me purity in His book, or He does not. He has either bought it for me, or He has not. It is either His will that I should be holy, or it is not. You know what He thinks and desires, and, oh! may faith be the conqueror. Trust Him and have the blessing, and you shall know it, and then like a dear friend, whom I hope we shall hear before the day has gone by, who went to the Mercy-seat, as we have begun to call it, at 101, Queen Victoria Street, where the Lord gave him the fulness of blessing, by not only showing him, but making him feel that the blood cleanseth. As he went off the platform, on Tuesday afternoon, at City Road Chapel, he said, "Mr. Booth, I think we have too much explaining. It is so simple. I feel that the blood of Christ can cleanse the whole world in a minute." I believe it too. I believe there is such a thing as so acting by faith or Divine power that when we come to exercise faith for the Holy Ghost we shall be able to rock the world. Oh! thou Omnipotent Jehovah, we have dishonoured Thee! We have dishonoured Thy power to save and conquer, and, above all, we have dishonoured that precious blood which Thy Son did shed. We have dishonoured it by limiting its power and cavilling about its cleansing efficacy. We will do it no longer. We will trust it. We will honour it by being cleansed. We will—Oh, blessed Lord, come and take possession of every soul in this building—do it now, and do it for ever. Amen and Amen.

The War Cry, No. 106.—Dec. 29, 1881.

CONSECRATION.

By W. BRAMWELL BOOTH.

Consecration is not Sanctification, for one is a condition of the other. Without a full surrendering to the will of God, and a full consecrating to the service of God, there cannot be full Salvation. And yet there may be a real giving up, a real forsaking of all, a real offering of ourselves to the Lord, and no more. So that some are fully consecrated who are not fully sanctified. Faith is the missing link.

When a man is seeking that God may wholly possess him, may wholly cleanse him, may purify and perfect him, and, seeking with his whole heart panting only for God, he will get clearer views of God's *requirements* than ever he had before. It is not a small thing, even to God, that He, the Lofty One, who inhabiteth eternity, whose name is Holy, should take up His abode in a man, and, on His account alone, are some things essential to be observed. He must be satisfied of one thing at least: that there is really no truce with his enemy, that there is really no, even neutral, ground left; that there is really and literally no reserve from Him of any sort. He will have *all*. He cannot let you cheat Himself, for His own sake as well as for yours. He must have all!

There is necessary, before you can be perfected in love,

1st, *A complete consecration to God's ownership;*

2nd, *A complete consecration to God's service.*

I observe that many seem to say to God when seeking a clean heart, "Oh! Lord, I give myself to Thee—my body, soul, and spirit. Drawn by Thy love, I lay my family and friends at Thy feet. I put my time, my gifts, my money at Thy disposal, lend them to me as Thy steward, or take them, some or all of them, from me as Thou wilt, they are Thine. My good name, my very joys, my past and present, and future, I offer Thee all, only Master, Thou wilt not take from me one thing,—*that*—Thou knowest it is not hurtful, and it is only a *little* matter, I cannot part with *that*, Thou shalt in reality have my all, *only*——!"

To such, God lends the hearing of supremest pity, but *He cannot cleanse what is not given.* A heart not wholly His own, how shall He sanctify? *Impossible.* By a service of *willing gift*, you *may* consecrate to His sole use your whole being, as Israel did that travelling Tabernacle in the wilderness, and be yourself a Temple for God to dwell in. But all must be given, for it must be all His own:

I have noticed, also, that the Holy Spirit of God does not stop here when leading souls to Canaan.

He requires also a genuine giving up to the *service* of God. To sacrifice to Him is good, to *obey is better*. Consecration unto Holiness means both. And many give God all they possess, all they have; they yield to Him with cheerful heart their most precious of all, filled with glad surprise that He should ask it of them, are glad to go bleeding and torn, to prove their love and faith. *They keep nothing back*. And when the Holy Ghost shows them that He asks a little more—the consecration of a lifetime to the *service* of God and souls—it may be to some service peculiarly and particularly painful, there is faltering and drawing back. Oh! Lord, anything but *that*. To go *there*. To be *this*. To endure that. I give Thee *all*, and I will do all, but I *can't* —— oh, Lord!"

And the *that* spoils all the rest. Ours is a jealous God. To Him consequences pleasant or painful do not count when He is *seeking His own*. He must have you to *possess*. He must have you wholly to *use*. I believe thousands blunder here. They seek Holiness for happiness sake, and never find. This necessary consecration to God's *service* from which they draw back in selfish haste, bars their way to *both*. For God cannot use what is not His, and He will not *take* from you in pretence what you do not offer Him in reality.

Know then, beloved, that Jesus is not a sham example, is not a mockery. To possess Him in saving, cleansing, healing power, in wisdom and righteousness, and full redemption, you must needs practically be no longer your own, but HIS, and further, must no longer seek or serve your own, but serve and seek THE THINGS THAT ARE JESUS CHRIST'S.

And we who have made with set purpose this twofold consecration, and have entered the land of rest, to prove that not one word of all our Lord's great promises has failed us there, but that all is come to pass, *we* have still to consecrate, not exactly after the fashion of which I have already spoken; bless God, that is over with us; is a wonderful unpulldownable reality of a fact in our lives. But there is a *third* consecration for us. We are to present our bodies a living sacrifice, HOLY, acceptable unto God. We are to go on ever, continually presenting to Him all we receive from Him, all we do for him, a holy offering, acceptable to Him. What honour, what joy. Here is our sacrifice always burning with holy fire of love, all we desire and do consecrated to Him, Sanctified to His glory, and accepted by Him.

Brother, sister, keep it up. The secret of continual getting is continual *giving*. Give God back again all you get. Glorify Him only by all you do. Never let Him need to ask you for aught. Be His own acceptable one. And your continual offering will be to Him a continual sweet-smelling savour, a joy to the conquering King Himself.

The War Cry, No. 144.—Sept. 21, 1882.

FIGHTING HOLINESS.

By MISS BOOTH, of Paris.

We often Sing—

> " We want no cowards in our band,
> Who from their colours fly ;"

and this is truer to-day than ever it was. Let it be known far and wide that the Salvation Army means war, and those who are not prepared for fighting, suffering, persecution, reproach, slander, a world's hatred, and all the rage of hell, are no good here ; no use applying.

If any people ought to be encouraged to fight we ought. Let us stop and think, for we are in danger of overlooking the goodness of our God. Who can describe the glorious victories that we have realized, The Red Seas crossed, the enemies put to flight? Who can sufficiently praise God for the thousands of souls we have captured from the devil? A great multitude has already crossed the river and entered the new city whose God is its light. (Our comrade Fry has just left us to help them sing.)

Who can tell of all the light, and peace, and joy that God has honoured us to bring into this dark world—the sins pardoned (what a multitude!), the guilty consciences relieved, the broken hearts healed, the tears wiped away, the prodigals returned, the homes made happy, the mothers' hearts made glad, the mourning turned into joy, and the spirits of heaviness exchanged for garments of praise?

Oh! methinks it would want ten thousand Eagles and Congress Halls, and then there would not be sufficient room to praise our God for what we have seen in the past. Truly, He who "led the children of Israel by the hand of Moses, with His glorious arm, dividing the water before them, to make Himself an everlasting name," hath led the Salvation Army by the right hand of our beloved General, dividing the waters before us to make Himself an everlasting name, which we will praise for ever and ever, throughout eternity.

And in view of all these great deliverances, miracles, and wonders that our God hath wrought among us: what manner of Soldiers ought we to be? How ought we to fight? How should we stand the fire? Is there anything in earth or hell that should be able to put Salvation Soldiers to flight?

I seem to hear a roar of voices reaching me across the Channel. "No, nothing! we will never run away."

But the great question that should occupy each one is, "How to fight so as to always ensure victory?"

1. See to it that you are pure in heart, that you leave no quarter for the enemy.

Remember you go out to denounce sin with a loud voice *in all its forms—Sin* dragging multitudes of deathless souls down to destruction—mind, then, that *you are delivered*, fully *delivered from it yourself*. (Here is the secret weakness of thousands, sin in the camp.) Mind, *if you would be strong in battle you must be pure in heart.*—Purity and power go together.

2. You must be saved from all secondary motives, from all wretched self-seeking, in all its wretched forms, from your miserable self altogether—Lost, dead to all but the interests of the war. Ready to do, to be, to dare anything to advance it; if your blood can serve, what higher honour could you have than to be counted worthy to shed it for such a cause. This must be your one and only end—your breath, your life.

3. Be prepared to meet the enemy. A man who goes unarmed to battle deserves to get wounded, and yet this is how thousands go into the Lord's battles. Is it any wonder that they get hurt? The instructions in the Book are plain enough on the subject. Then "Quit yourselves like men; be strong." "Put on the whole armour of God."

Be ready to face the foe, and then when the shots of the devil come flying in all directions, you will not be taken by surprise. Darkness, persecution, reproach, and sorrow will come—*must come*—just in proportion as you follow your Lord, and are faithful to your colours. Do you choose an easier path than your Saviour trod? Nay, there is only one road to save the world, and that is the road by Calvary. Then expect the treatment of your Lord, and be ready armed like a true warrior to meet it. Then, when the enemy shall come in like a flood; when the thunders roar, and everything looks black, you will be able to stand your ground, and be more than a match for the devil. This *is* war! It is not likely the devil is going to let us go at this express rate without doing his very utmost to hinder. Oh! how he hates us? So you who are in the thickest of the fight; you, who are pressed sore on every hand, look up! be of good courage; hold on. Remember, it is wonderfully true that—

"Jesus is a rock in a weary land,
A shelter in the time of storm."

Sing it again! and let your weakness lean on His might. He knows your every struggle, and is ever near to strengthen, to comfort even as a mother comforteth. Go on fighting! there's a glorious victory ahead for you.

Forward! my comrades, faster than ever before! there never was a time when there was such a call for Soldiers who know how to fight—not a day, a month, a year, but right to the end with a desperate earnestness, and a courage that cannot be daunted. Let the devil do his worst, we know he is a conquered foe. To arms! ye brave, to take the world!

Paris, September, 11*th,* 1882.

The War Cry, No. 85.—Aug. 4, 1881.

REPRESSION

IS NOT

SANCTIFICATION.

By Rev. DANIEL STEELE, D.D.

It is my purpose to clearly set forth several insuperable objections to that definition of entire sanctification which makes it consist in the power of the Holy Spirit repressing inbred sin, choking down the old man instead of crucifying him till he is stone dead.

1. Our first objection is, that it does not harmonize with the consciousness of entirely sanctified persons. These testify with Arvid Gradin to "the highest tranquility, serenity, and peace of mind, with a deliverance from every fleshly desire, and a cessation of all, even inward, sin."

We admit that if we are entirely passive in sanctification, we might not be conscious of this repressive force, holding in check our sinful proclivities. But it is a principle of the great scheme of gospel salvation to employ the agency of the subject. He is to be a co-worker with God. Hence he would be conscious of his share in the work of repression, even if he were not conscious of the work performed by the Spirit.

The uniform testimony is to a delightful sense of inward purity, the absence of all risings of malice, envy, and self-seeking. Now, if all these still exist within, but only neutralized by a superior force crushing them down, consciousness must attest to a falsehood when she bears witness to entire inward purity.

2. Lack of a scriptural basis. It is a remarkable fact that while the Greek language richly abounds in words signifying repression, a half score of which occur in the New Testament, and are translated by *to bind, bruise, cast down, conquer, bring into bondage, let, repress, hold fast, hinder, restrain, subdue, put down*, and *take by the throat*, yet not one of these is used of inbred sin; but such verbs as signify to cleanse, to purify, to mortify or kill, to crucify, and to destroy. When St. Paul says that he keeps under his body, and brings it into subjection, he makes no allusion to the flesh, the carnal mind, but to his innocent bodily appetites. In Pauline usage *body* is different from *flesh*. We have diligently sought in both the Old Testament and the New for exhortations to seek the repression of sin. The uniform command is to put away sin, to purify the heart, to purge out the old leaven, and to seek to be sanctified throughout soul, body, and spirit. Repressive power is nowhere ascribed to the blood of Christ, but rather purgative efficacy. Now, if

these verbs, which signify to cleanse, wash, crucify, mortify, or make dead, and to destroy, are all used in a typical or metaphorical sense, it is very evident that the literal truth signified is something far stronger than repression. It is eradication, extinction of being, destruction.

3. The repressive theory of Holiness is out of harmony with the Divine purity. Holiness in man must mean precisely the same as Holiness in God, who announces Himself as holy, and then founds human obligation to Holiness upon this revealed attribute: "Be ye holy, FOR I AM HOLY." Who dares to say that God's Holiness is different from man's Holiness, save that the one is original, and the other is in-wrought by the Holy Ghost?

Well does one say, "How can a man even know what is meant by justice in the Deity, if there is absolutely nothing of the same species in his own rational constitution, which, if realized in his own character as it is in that of God, would make him just as God is just? If there is no part of man's complex being, upon which he may fall back with the certainty of not being mistaken in his judgment of ethics and religion, then are both anchor and anchorage gone, and he is afloat upon the boundless, starless ocean of ignorance and scepticism."

Who can confidently adore, and sincerely love a being who may, in the inmost essence of his being, be pure malignity in the outward guise of benevolence? Now, if Holiness in man is the same kind as Holiness in God—and it is perilous to deny it—what becomes of the repressive theory?

Are there explosive elements in the Divine

nature, and is there some outside power holding down sinful tendencies in His heart? Or is He Himself holding them down? Let St. John answer, "In Him is no darkness"—moral evil—"at all." His nature is unmingled purity. This must be the pattern of our Holiness. "He that hath this hope in Him purifieth himself, EVEN AS HE IS PURE."

4. Our next objection to this theory is, that it confounds the distinction between Holiness and virtue. We never call God virtuous, nor angels, nor Jesus Christ, nor the spirits of the just made perfect, whether in the body or out of the body. We do not magnify, but rather belittle the Son of God to ascribe to Him only virtue. He is holy, harmless, undefiled, separate from sinners. What is the specific difference between virtue and Holiness? Repression. Virtue is the triumph of right against strong inward tendencies toward the opposite. Jesus triumphed over outward temptations to sin, and was holy. Mary Magdalene by divine grace triumphed over inward tendencies toward vice, and was virtuous. The repressive theory of Holiness, involving, as it must, the co-working of the human soul with the Divine Represser, confounds the broad distinction between Holiness and virtue, and banishes Holiness from the earth, substituting virtue instead. In fact, we do not see any possibility, on this theory, for a fallen man ever to become holy, in the sense of the entire extinction of inbred sin. If this is only repressed here, it may be only repressed for ever hereafter. If the Holy Spirit cannot eradicate original sin now, through faith in the blood of Jesus, what assurance have

we that He can ever entirely sanctify our souls? But if by repression is meant the right poising of the innocent passions of sanctified human nature after the extinction of ingratitude, unbelief, malice, self-will, and every other characteristic of depraved human nature which is sinful of itself, we accept it as Scriptural.

The War Cry, No. 153.—Oct. 26, 1882.

COME TO THE POINT.

An Address at the Congress Hall, Clapton, October 12th, 1882.

By MISS BOOTH, of Paris.

MISS BOOTH, from Paris, whose rising produced a great demonstration, said:—I was very much struck with what the General just now said to us about an examination. He said it would be well for us to have a time, perhaps once a-week, to pull ourselves up, to look into our own hearts and find out where we stand in the sight of God, and in the view of eternity. I say, Amen to that. I would that every Soldier in the Salvation Army adopted that plan—that we once a-week pulled ourselves up face to face with the light—and if we do, God will teach us great things. He will reveal unto us His will, and we shall be able to do it. You know there are things that God does reveal, such as Major Corbridge was referring to this evening, things that when people come to our meetings *do* come up before them. They at other times put their hands before their eyes, and refuse to see them. The next Friday night, or the next person they meet who belongs to the Salvation Army, they come up again; but they turn their heads, they don't want to face the question. Now I do not know a greater folly. I do not know a greater fool, spiritually speaking, than a man who does like that with his conscience, and with those things in his heart and in his life, that are not in accordance with the will of God. Oh! what folly to put these things on one side, to throw the matter over, as thousands of the people do, into a world of indefiniteness, and begin talking (to smother a guilty conscience) about "growing in grace!" There is no such thing as growing while that is the case. There is wanted a private examination. Oh! yes, there is something wrong, and you must bring yourself up to the light now. Is it so? Through these meetings, perhaps, while we were singing,

"Take all my sins away,

on our knees, perhaps during the chorus embodying that beautiful answer—

"Yes, Lord, I will be thine!"

something came up to stand between your soul and God. Has the Holy Spirit again brought up this old controversy that has appeared over, and over, and over again, only you have never been brave enough, man enough, so to speak, to face the question and SETTLE IT, but you have put it on one side month after month, year after year—is it again uppermost to-night? God knows if it is. By-and-bye, what a revelation! what an agony! what an *eternal shame* will cover thousands of professing Christians when in the Last Great Day this old point is brought up before Him in whom neither dwelleth changeableness nor the shadow of turning! He knows all about it. When before His throne there comes up that point, little and trivial though you think it is, which has kept you out of light, blessing, power, holiness, that you will only be able to measure the worth of in the light of eternity, when you see the long dark army of souls passing down to the bottomless pit.

"*Little!*"—you call it;—"BIG"—HE calls it. It is sin, and it comes between your soul and Him—whether it be a pipe, or dress, or drink, or society, or anything else. It is to you SIN—it is doubtful—the least you can say. Now will you continue in it? Will you go on? or will you say—"By the grace of God this night, in this Hall, on this 12th of October, I will settle that matter between God and my own soul for ever?"

DRAG YOUR SOUL UP!

I will drag my soul up, I will say—

"Come here soul, you have flinched and shrunk from the knife, but I will know the truth; I will know what God thinks about you. Come here. I will drag you up, if you bleed at every pore; if it costs you your blood; if it means sacrifice, and suffering, and real crucifixion; if it does MEAN THE NAILS! I will suffer the loss of all things, but this one thing shall be settled. I will be right with God and in harmony with Him and my conscience.

and my life, and my heart shall be all in unison with His will."

You settle that there is light and peace for you. There is a life of power for you. There are precious souls for you; yea, you shall be the mothers and the fathers of a Spiritual Israel, and you shall see hundreds saved. Will you do that? Will you come up to that point?

Make no mistake—God is not cheated. People who are not honest and straightforward with God, God knows all about it, and keeps account. I am very glad they do *not* get all they want; that they do not save their lives because they do not go in for the losing of them. It is they that lose their lives and say, "I am willing to be crucified, unknown, despised, and rejected, and shut up—I am willing to do all that." They are the people that God rejoices in. Regarding such people, God says—

"You angels stand aside. I will wipe all tears away from their eyes; I will crown them; I will say 'well done' to them, and they shall lack no good thing."

They lose their lives, and they find them every day—a hundred fold. We experience this. Poor and despised as we are, we are the richest lot of people under Heaven. (Volley.)

Why They Can't Hurt Us.

The papers and people writing against us! I said to a lady the other day,

"Do you think they hurt us? My dear woman, I praise God morning, noon, and night for it, because I am so glad. I say Hallelujah! in my inmost soul."

It is a grand chance for our work in Paris. At last we have reached the climax of the English war. and at last we have gained the grand eminence of suffering persecution. The papers begin to blacken us, and ever since they have done so we have gone rolling along more rapidly than before. This does not hurt us.

Why doesn't it hurt us? Because we have gone in for losing all! Our reputation, our comfort, our ease, our miserable puny interests, God forbid that any one particle, the least degree of self-seeking, should exist among us. God crucify us out and out, throughout all our borders, and then indeed we shall be a people, as Commissioner Railton said, and that is a profound thought—that thought is worthy of your thinking about—not only now as God has so honoured us, only through our being willing to go down, as our Lord went down, and accept the cross, and the thorns, and the blood—he said that not only shall we go on as we have done, but make such an impression that he believed the whole world would be won for Christ. (Volley.) I believe it in my soul. (Volley.) I believe America and India—the Lord bless India, that has just started—and Australia, and our darling France, will be won! France, with those infidels and *libres penseurs*, and the people who say they don't believe in anything at all—I believe that a great army shall be raised up in all nations of the earth, that shall go forth and take all before them. Why? Because, thank God, we have gone in for the losing. We say we are content to lose; we do not care for ourselves, we have adopted the principle of John the Baptist—"I must decrease, but He must increase."

THE SECRET OF VICTORY.

Oh! there is the secret of success and power. People say to me, "I have no power." No wonder, I repeat. I am glad they have not got power. They do not pay the price; but we who pay the price, God pays us back again in profits. He gives us increase. We have gone in for the losing, and we are in for the finding. Just one word more. That person of whom I have been talking, who comes up to the light again and again—whatever it is, in your own conscience, that is standing between you and God, and keeping you out of the Kingdom—you know that that is destroying your influence and marring your peace. Every time such a man goes back, his case is a harder case. His conscience becomes more seared, and I know nothing on earth or in Heaven, nothing is there, I maintain, in the universe, so sad and so awful to bear, that makes such a hell in a man's bosom, as a guilty conscience. And, oh! if a guilty conscience in a sinner is so awful and so hard to bear, what is it with those who have received the light, and know God's will, but do it not? What is it with those who have sat under teaching as clear as the noon-day sun—who have understood so well, that, if all the angels in Heaven had come to explain, you could not understand better just what God wants of you? You have seen as clearly as anybody can see; you know very well what is wanted of you, and all the time you hold back. Oh! what a conscience that is!—oh! what a burden!—oh! what a hell that will make if it goes on like this, if this binding up of the leg goes on, you saying, "I don't want to see what is the matter, and I won't face the question."

Mortification sets in—spiritual *mortification* and *that means death!* It means the departure of the Holy Spirit; it means, "That is enough; I have striven with the man long—days, and weeks, and months, and years. I have stretched out My hand I have given him the light. I have given him everything but he has persistently refused me." Oh! the reproach and the agony of the guilty conscience in the judgment day, in looking back on all this. Oh! you people in England, my soul trembles for your responsibility, you, who are flooded with light, you, who know all about the truth, and you, who know your Bibles from end to end. Oh! you people, you people, how responsible are you? If I were on my death-bed, I think I should turn round to you and say, "Oh! if you could but understand for one half hour, if in your little puny souls you were to become so large as to understand the worth of precious souls around you, and your awful responsibility in the sight of God, you would shriek out, and stand up in this audience as one man and say, from this hour I will be entirely the Lord's; I will be willing to lose my life, and I will be willing to crucify myself. I will give my life for a dying world." But you do not. You are slow and stupefied. Will you remain so? Will you not do right? Will you not come up to the point, and say, "I will?" Will you not do it now? Will you not do it this evening? this blessed solemn hour, for He lives to take AWAY YOUR SINS as well as mine. I can say, to the honour and glory of God, that in Paris, in most respects, a weary land for me, God has been my rock and my Salvation! I do like to say it to His glory that He has sustained me, and in hours of terrible trial when every thing has seemed black as night, God has kept my eyes fixed on Him, and has given me the desire of my heart in the Salvation of souls. He is able to do that for me, because I believe I can say there is not a desire or a thought in my whole being but for His glory and the interest of His kingdom, and if He does that for *me* He is able to do that for you, also every one in this Hall. Shall it be so? When?

This was followed up in a proper, practical way by a call for instant surrender. It was impossible to get people forward in the crowded Hall. But they were asked to stand up whilst, in prayer and song, we all offered ourselves once more to God, or whilst in a still grander

SILENCE, WITH 10,000 EYES SHUT,

we each and all talked with God. Oh! what a time that Evening Meeting was. Again and again, from the first song to the end, it seemed to us one of the most wonderful meetings of God and man that ever took place.

Before that clear light there could be no excuse, and oh, surely many a soul did truly draw nigh to God, and receive such light and power as they had never had before. We have no idea how many stood up, as it was a real prayer-meeting, with at least 10,000 eyes shut, whilst it seemed as though every soul was drawing nigh to God. Yes, that was a glorious wedding-day, and if everyone did not go away in the spirit of Major Smith's closing song,

"Ever ready, night or day,
To fire away,"

it must have been entirely their own fault.

The War Cry, No. 82.—July 14, 1881.

LET GO AND TRUST.

By Rev. DANIEL STEELE, D.D.

It is an inspiring thought that we are addressing a multitude of readers who would know more of Christ. A languid desire is not sufficient. You must desire Jesus with an intensity which will make your soul a glowing furnace. You must reach the point where you will be willing to sell all, or hold all else cheap in comparison with the fulness of love to Christ.

There are but two steps which lead down into the pool which makes whole—consecration and trust. Difficulties attend both steps. Some are in doubt whether they surrender all to the disposal of Christ. To such we say, "Consecrate all you know, and then all you do not know." This includes all your assets. God asks no more than this. At this point many fail, through fear that they are to become paupers, when God means to endow them with untold wealth. What, let Christ become my Lord indeed? Is it safe to give Him complete control over my heart, to be the sovereign of my will, the owner of all my property, while I sink down to a mere stewardship under Him! Will He not take some cruel advantage of me? Will He not command me to hard service? Will not reproaches be heaped upon me, if I avow before men and angels that I am wholly Christ's? Very likely He will honour you by entrusting to you some difficult labour. If you go into partnership with Him you must share all the reproach which comes upon the firm. You are advised beforehand that Jesus is an unpopular character in what is called the best society.

"If they have called the master of the house Beelzebub, how much more so shall they call them of his household?" "The world will hate you because it hateth Me; be but of good cheer, for I have overcome the world." Hence there can be no perfect consecration without an accompanying perfect trust.

Just here let us whisper in your ear, that perfect reliance on Christ is impossible, so long as you are cherishing your good name as a treasure more precious than His glory. I think that He had ministers of His Gospel especially in view when He said, "How can ye believe which receive honour one of another, and seek not the honour that cometh from God only?" This is not a rebuke for a jealous care of our moral standing, since an untarnished name is, with preachers, an indispensable condition of success, but for a weak truckling to a public opinion, hostile to unadulterated Christian truth. They are tempted to temporize and tone down the

Gospel to please men on whom they think themselves dependent. Reader, your reputation is not too good to give to the Lord Jesus. Paul's self-surrender included his popularity. "If I yet pleased men, I should not be the servant of Christ."

It is true, also, that far more of consecration succeeds the act of perfect faith and realized sanctification than precedes it. Under the full blaze of the Spirit's illumination, we see much more to consecrate than we did before.

"But," says one, "I cannot see God's hand; how, then, can I know that He accepts the offering of my heart?" You are not required to know, but to believe.

"How can I believe when I feel no change?" The ground of your faith must not be your feelings, but the Word of God. When you make a legal tender of yourself to Him, it is your duty to believe that He accepts you according to His promise. This is simple faith. When it pleases God He will give to your soul a joyful realization of your acceptance. This is knowledge. The Divine order, both in nature and in grace, is faith, the stepping-stone to knowledge.

If the blessing of conscious completeness in Christ, and the abiding Comforter and Sanctifier is by faith only, why not now? To-day is the day of salvation. Full salvation surrounds you like a shoreless ocean. Appropriate to your utmost capacity to-day. You will gain nothing by waiting. There is no lack for God to supplement, and there is no particular in which you can improve yourself and make yourself more acceptable to Him.

Neither sanctification or justification is by works. Works involve the element of time: but faith says, "Now, this instant, Thou, oh, God, wilt receive my offering."

"But," says doubt, "Suppose that I feel just the same after I thus believe, what then?"

Keep on believing the promise, and insisting that God is true. He may delay for days and weeks the declaration of your complete acceptance, in order to develop and test your faith. The longer the delay, if you trust unwaveringly, the more marvellous the manifestation of Christ to your soul as your complete Saviour, when the Comforter takes the things of Christ, and shows them unto you. The Syrophenician woman lost nothing by pressing her suit against chilling discouragements. Faint not. Just here thousands have failed. They did not grasp the prize because they did not persistently believe.

Others fail through a subtle legality. They trust in their consecration, and not in Jesus only. They take a commercial view of the matter, and present the offering of their hearts as the meritorious ground of receiving the fulness of the Spirit. This is a piece of folly and presumption which finds its parallel in the way-side beggar, who insists that the act of stretching out his upturned palm earns the alms which the passer-by may give.

After you have laid your gift upon the altar, look away from the gift, that is now God's, towards the skies, whence the fire shall come down to consume the sacrifice, in token of its acceptance. Thus, in all our approaches to God there are three things requisite—Belief, Faith, Trust. "For He that cometh to God must believe that He is, and that He is the rewarder of them that diligently seek Him."

I sat me down on earth's benighted vale,
 And had no courage and no strength to rise,
ad to the passing breeze I told my tale,
 And bowed my head and drained my weeping eyes.

But faith came by and took me by the hand
 And now the valleys rise and mountains fall;
Welcome the stormy sea, the boisterous land,
 With faith to aid me I can conquer all.

The War Cry, No. 122.—April 20, 1882.

NO TRUCE WITH GIBEON.

NOTES OF AN ADDRESS AT THE ALL-NIGHT-OF-PRAYER AT WHITECHAPEL.

By MAJOR TUCKER
(Of the Indian Division).

WHILST listening to Major Howard, to-night, I was examining myself, and I am thankful to be able to testify now, that my will is in complete submission to the will of God; that I have a conscience void of offence towards God and man, and my heart seems filled with love alone. Of all the different aspects of Sanctification, I love to think especially of entire Purity. Oh, it is glorious to know that Christ is able to keep us blameless, and to present us before the Father without spot or wrinkle, or any such thing. Last Thursday, one of the Soldiers at Chalk Farm was describing how, when his heart was cleansed from sin, he gave up smoking, and so determined was he to have done with it for ever, that he would not even wear one of his coats which smelt of tobacco till his wife had washed it. Not satisfied with that, he gave it a good rinsing himself to make sure that there was no trace of smell left about it. And I thought, yes, that is Scriptural. We are taught to hate even the garment spotted by the flesh. But alas! alas! this is just where so many fail. Their garments are tainted with the world. It may be that they have only a few streaks of worldliness, but there it is. It may be that they have gone further and have got a fringe of the spirit of the world, or even a broad band, whilst others are spotted and speckled all over. Thank God it is our privilege—it is God's command that we should have and keep our garments unspotted by the flesh, and if the Spirit of God has been showing us that such is not our state, we may have the blood applied, and be cleansed from all our filthiness to-night.

When the Israelites were entering the Promised Land, God commanded them to exterminate all the inhabitants, and expressly forbade them ever to make a league with them. God never commands impossibilities, and, in this case, He promised them special help to enable them to destroy their enemies. He said that He would send His hornets before them, so that they would be able to win an easy victory wherever they went. Of course hornets are much more common in the East than they are in our country, and some of my friends have told me of the narrow escapes that they have had, where a nest was accidently disturbed.

Well, I can imagine I see a band of the Israelite soldiers, set in array, down at the foot of some steep hill. Look, there at the top are the Anakites or the Amalekites. You can see giants among them, seven, eight, or nine feet tall; they have all the advantage of position, and, very likely, of numbers too. What can that handful of Israelites do? But, Joshua leads the way, and on they go in the name of the Lord. And, suddenly, while their enemies are preparing to rush down upon them, and sweep them off the hill-side, buzz came a swarm of hornets round their ears. Imagine the confusion that would follow in the camp. Imagine their frantic efforts to drive off these new enemies. But the hornets only swarm the thicker over their faces, and hands, and bodies, till they lie rolling on the ground in an agony of pain. Meanwhile the Israelites are at the top, they have no battle to fight, they have but to slay their already helpless enemies. Oh, dear friends, this is just what God has promised to do for you. Do you see that Anak of Temper, of Pride, of Self? You have fired your good resolutions at it time after time, but there it is as strong as ever. Now, in the name of the Lord, close with the foe. His hornets will go before you, the enemy will be helpless before you can come up with him, and you will have but to slay him and fling his carcase over the walls.

What a grand chance the Israelites had of destroying all their enemies, when God was so wonderfully helping them! What a pity that they did not avail themselves of it! No, they began to slacken their efforts before long. The plausible Gibeonites easily caught them in a trap, and Israel soon began to find out that it was much more convenient to make tributaries of the nations than to extirpate them. Yes, it was very nice to have those Gibeonites as hewers of wood, and drawers of water. What a lot of trouble it saved them; instead of going away to the well, or the stream to fetch water, and instead of having to climb the mountains for their wood, they had only to send off a Gibeonite, and he would gladly do it for them. Then gradually we find that, instead of making their enemies tributaries, they dwelt among them, and then intermarried with them, and served their gods. Finally, they seemed to throw off religion altogether, and we read that every man did that which was pleasing in his own eyes. Is not this an exact picture of many present here this evening? Can you not remember the time, when in the warmth of your first love, you were ready to uproot and destroy every sin, and were determined never to give them any quarter. But after a time your efforts began to slacken, you grew weary of the slaughter. Satan persuaded you that there was no necessity for you to hound down every sin that might be discovered. You began by sparing their lives, and making them tributaries. They seemed so harmless and inoffensive at first, but now, alas; they have come to be your masters, and you have vainly struggled for deliverance from the galling yoke which they have fixed upon your neck. But, oh, Hallelujah! the Deliverer is here to-night? He will save you out of the hand of your enemies. Will you let Him? Will you come to Him that He may sprinkle you with water? and you shall be clean. He will wash you, and you shall be whiter than snow.

The War Cry, No. 123.—April 27, 1882.

POWER WANTED.

THE SUBSTANCE OF

AN EXETER HALL ADDRESS,

By THE GENERAL.

As to the desirability of this task, the destruction of evil, of which we have been speaking, there will be in this Hall I should think this morning scarcely two opinions. Indeed, with many, an almost constant sense of the desirability of such a condition and course of conduct as that we have described is constantly present. They can see the blessedness of the state, and long to have it in their possession. They are always looking over Jordan, and pronouncing it to be a good land. They receive the report of the spies and those who have been over and walked about it, but they themselves have been held back from any real attempt to cross over and possess, and enjoy the goodly land by a feeling of inability to overcome their inbred foes, or maintain the benefits if they could be attained. There is, perhaps, no passage of Scripture the truthfulness of which they more fully realised in their own consciences, than that which says, "Of myself I can do nothing." What they want is to finish the quotation in their own faith and realisation. "I can do all things through Christ, which strengtheneth me." They want power.

It seems to me that just now there is a great waking up on every hand to desire a higher type of Christianity, and yet there is a corresponding feeling of the need of power to realise it. I want this yearning after power to be increased, and then there will be some probability of this realisation.

There is a great hungering after power just now among the philosophers in the natural and scientific world. They want a new motive power to supersede steam; or, at least, they say they have discovered the power in electricity. They say it is all there, equal to all their desires, but they want some cheap and easy method of utilising it. There is the power, they are sure of it. It is all around them everywhere, but they want to throw their reins around its neck, fasten it to their machinery, and make it serve their interests and do their work and will. So here, my comrades, who are hungering and thirsting after spiritual power, oh, what a mighty task wants doing, and after all, how little is being done. As I go about, looking at the public poison trees that grow in no secret places, where wholesale and retail poisoning is done; when I think what breaking of hearts, and blighting of futures, and marring of souls is done in this vast city alone, to say nothing of all the dark places of the earth, how my heart aches. Oh, what mountains of difficulty there are in the way of the Salvation of this city, and of the other cities of the world. What can we do? This can't be the end contemplated by Jehovah and by Calvary? My soul, as well as your Bible, answers "No!" Ten thousand times "No!" But how do better? There is power, plenty of power, oceans of power. Latterly I have seemed to feel it very near. Thank God for the measure of it we have. It has wrought wonderful deliverances for many of us personally, and, through us, He has worked deliverance to tens of thousands more, but there is more at hand—power to shake London, Paris, and the world. Let us unite to have it.

But, my friends, is there not power for you to fight the evil of which we have just been speaking; you have tried mental power, you have tried intellectual power, you have heard the most marvellous discourses and disquisitions ever delivered on this subject, you have tried all sorts of power; now just come and try Divine power—the Almighty power of God, and see if there shall not be done for you just what you need.

Now, mark here, firstly, *you have not in any shape or form to generate this power.* They talk about generating electricity, but by generation they don't mean creation. They cannot generate or manufacture as much electricity as would kill a fly or illuminate a cellar. They can only, by some kind of machinery, take hold of that electricity which God has generated, which is all about us, focus it, and bring it to bear upon the work they want to be done. We have been thinking of lighting up our new building at Clapton with the electric light; but they want £400 for such a machine, and consequently, as we have not the money, we must do without it. Now, in your experience, you want something analagous to this generator, that is, you want that faith that will bring the Divine power—the Heavenly electricity—down upon your will, destroy the evil tendencies out of your nature, making you the master of your appetites and purposes, so that all shall be directed and managed for the glory of God, and the good of men.

Secondly,—You will have to get this power direct from God Himself. In electricity they have got a plan of storing it up, and sending it about the country. For instance, they can have some great central manufacturing or generating force, and in this way the Americans are proposing to utilise the Falls of Niagara, and from this great source sending out "power" all over the country. I suppose you would read something of this kind having been done as a commencement; a jar of this electric power was sent from Paris to Edinburgh, by which some celebrated surgeon there performed a remarkable operation. Now there is no method of this description by which you can obtain a stock of Divine power to accomplish the end you have in view. You must obtain it direct from the great Master Himself. You can't go to some Holiness Council and there obtain a stock of power to last until another Council comes round. It is true that a man can be so stirred up at our gatherings to acts of faith that he shall carry away a heart full of love and power with which he shall go forth and do wonderful things. But then, he obtains it from Jehovah Himself, and must *go on obtaining it in the same way*, if he is to go on having it. You must, with your own hand of faith, obtain from God, and bring down into your own soul, this power for the destruction and mastery over evil. Do you say, "How is it to be done?" That passage which I read over describes the method. Here it is: "Have faith in God!"

I remember when I was a boy one of my school-fellows taking me into his father's works. It was the first time I had seen any machinery, and the moving engine and machines filled my young mind with wonder. He then created a still greater amount of wonder by taking a piece of iron and fixing it to a lathe, and then by pushing a rod he connected the powerless lathe with the powerful engine, and immediately round went the wheels of the lathe, and the piece of iron he had fixed on it was cut as easily as if it had been a piece of wood, to my utter amazement. Now, you say, "I am struggling with my temper, I have fought my pride, I have fought all the evils of my nature which rule me with a rod of iron; I have read books about them, heard sermons preached about them, I have struggled thus for weeks until I am clean in despair, and after all I have done I am helpless and powerless in the matter." Perfectly true, is all you say; you are helpless of yourself, but He is Almighty to save you. Make the connection with the Omnipotent Engine that drives the universe. You want the link that connects your helplessness with His Almightiness. That link is "faith." "Have faith in God."

But someone says "I have heard you before in this hall and elsewhere, say there are other conditions to this full Salvation." Yes, you have heard me say that before a man can be cleansed from sin he must be willing to give up sin, and to renounce all those ways and habits about the rightness or wrongness of which he has reason to doubt, in other words, he must be willing, for God, to make, and save, and keep him a holy man. I say that. I have said it before, and I say it again, and I say further, as I have said on this platform before, that God can't give a man His full Salvation till that man is willing to follow Him wheresoever He leadeth. He must be willing to sink his own will. If God says, "I want you to live in Australia," he must be willing to go and live in Australia. If you want to be a saint, you must be willing to be a saint; but someone says, "You said just now, that faith was the one condition that connected man with this Divine and Omnipotent power;" yes! because these two conditions are only other aspects and attitudes of faith. Faith says, "My Master, my Saviour, my Holy King, I see and admire Thy Holy will; I embrace it. I turn round from all other things. I drop them as a child who is playing with the scissors, when the mother gives it a beautiful shell, drops the scissors and takes the shell. I will give up all to God and follow Him fully, to be one of the angels that stand in His presence, who always do the will of Him that sits upon the Throne. I will always do the will of Him that sits upon the Throne, although I live in Whitechapel, whether I run, or walk the streets, or ride in a coach to do it. 'Have faith in God.' 'Have faith in God.'"

This is the rod that will bring the electricity into your heart, I have seen, as you all have, on the steeples of churches, and on the high chimneys of factories, a rod fixed on the side, they call it "*a lightning conductor.*" What is it for? It is there to break the overhanging lightning-cloud, and convey the electricity, safely, and harmlessly into the earth. Now, there are some people who have got up alongside them an electric rod, a sort of lightning conductor, which when God's lightnings are floating about in Exeter Hall, and other times of great and glorious visitation, instead of conveying this electricity *into* their own hearts, takes it from them, that is, passes it away. They have some sort of fear, or feeling, or doctrine, or text of Scripture, or an opinion of man, or something which carries the lightning off them, and leaves them as they were before. You want the rod of simple faith, it will catch the cloud, and bring the electricity into your souls. Now, then, up with the rod, catch the living power, never mind, what it wrecks, breaks down, or drives away. If you have anything that God is against, let it be broken and smashed in pieces. He is going to be the King—whatever there is about you that He doesn't like, will have to be smashed, you will have to be saved from sin and sinning, or you will never go into the glory land. When this is done by the mighty power of God through the blood of His precious

Son, and to the glory of His name, you will have complied with the conditions, the giving up of evil and presenting yourself to God and the believing that God does save you according to His word, then it will be done, and, when it is done, God will begin to adorn you because He wants you for His dwelling-place. The Heaven of Heavens is His town house, but the hearts of His contrite ones are His country home. He will come and live in your heart all the year round, giving you joy and plenty. He will manifest Himself in His glory, will tell you His secrets, and you shall have no more fears, you shall be ministers of righteousness, flames of fire, of whom the world shall feel the power, and His name shall be glorified for ever.

The War Cry, No. 126.—MAY 18, 1882.

MADAME GUYON'S EXPERIENCE.

From the POPULAR PENNY BIOGRAPHY, *To be had at every Station of the Army.*

"GREAT was the change which I had now experienced; but still, in my exterior life, I appeared to others quite simple, unobstrusive, and common; and the reason was, that my soul was not only brought into harmony with itself and with God, but with God's providences. In the exercise of faith and love, I endured and performed whatever came in God's providence, in submission, in thankfulness, and silence. I was now in God, and God in me; and where God is there is as much simplicity as power. And what I did was done in such simplicity and childlikeness of spirit, that the world did not observe anything which was much calculated to attract notice.

I had a deep peace which seemed to pervade the whole soul, and resulted from the fact that all my desires were fulfilled in God. I feared nothing; that is, considered in its *ultimate results and rela-*

tions, because my strong faith placed God at the head of all perplexities and events. I desired nothing but what I now had, because I had a full belief that, in my present state of mind, the results of each moment constituted the fulfilment of the Divine purposes. As a sanctified heart is always in harmony with the Divine Providences, I had no will but the Divine will, of which such providences are the true and appropriate expression. How could such a soul have other than a deep peace, not limited to the uncertainties of the emotional part of our nature, but which pervaded and blessed the whole mind! Nothing seemed to diminish it; nothing troubled it.

I do not mean to say that I was in a state in which I could not be afflicted. My physical system, my senses, had not lost the power of suffering My natural sensibilities were susceptible of being pained. Oftentimes I suffered much. But in the centre of the soul, if I may so express it, there was Divine and supreme peace. The soul, considered in its connection with the objects immediately around it, might at times be troubled and afflicted? but the soul, considered in its relation to God and the Divine will, was entirely calm, trustful, and happy. The trouble at the circumference, originating in part from a disordered physical constitution, did not affect and disturb the Divine peace of the centre.

One characteristic of this higher degree of experience was a sense of inward purity. *My mind had such a oneness with God*, such a unity with the Divine nature, that nothing seemed to have power to soil it and to diminish its purity. It experienced the truth of that declaration of Scripture, that "to the pure all things are pure." The pollution which surrounds has no power upon it; as the dark and impure mud does not defile the sunbeams that shine upon it, which rather appear brighter and purer from the contrast.

But though I was so much blessed, I was not conscious of any merit, nor tempted by any suggestions of merit in myself. Indeed, I seemed to be so united with God, so made one with the centre and sum of all good, that my thoughts did not easily turn upon myself as a distinct object of reflection ? and, consequently, it would not have been an easy thing for me to attach to myself the idea of merit. If I had done virtuously and meritoriously by a *laborious effort*, the idea of merit would more naturally and readily have suggested itself, and I might have been tempted to indulge thoughts of that kind. But now that God had become the inward operator, and every movement was a movement originating, as it were, in a Divine inspiration, and as a holy life had become as natural to me as the life of nature formerly had been, I could not well attribute to myself what evidently belonged to God. To Him, and to Him only, to His goodness and His grace, I attributed all worthiness, all praise.

It was one of the characteristics of my experience at this time, that I could not move myself, or bring myself into action, from the principle of self, because self was gone. I stood silent and unmoved in the midst of God's providences, until the time of movement came, which was indicated by these providences. Then I decided when God called me to decide, and with God to help me to decide.

From this time I found myself in the enjoyment of liberty. My mind experienced a remarkable facility in doing and suffering everything which presented itself in the order of God's providence. God's order became its law. In fulfilling this law, it experienced no inward repugnance, but fulfilled its own highest wishes, and therefore could not but be conscious of the highest inward liberty. When the soul loses the limit of selfishness,—a limit which fixes the soul in itself,—it has no limit but in God, who is without limits. What limit, then, can be placed to the length and breadth of its freedom?"

God had tried, and purified, and prepared her for great things, using her all the while as a light to lighten the darkness of many; but now He was about to lead her forth to do greater things by far. She was puzzled as to whether it would be right for her to leave her children in order to be free for public service, and God answered her in a very remarkable way.

"I was obliged," she says, "to go to Paris about some business. Having entered into a church that was very dark, I went up to the first confessor I found there. I had never seen him before, and have never seen him since. I made a simple and short confession; but with the confessor himself, aside from the religious act, I did not enter into conversation. And accordingly, he surprised me much in saying of his own accord, 'I know not who you are, whether maid, wife, or widow? but I feel a strong inward emotion to exhort you to do what the Lord has made known to you that He requires of you. I have nothing else to say.'"

I answered him, "Father, I am a widow, who have little children. What else could God require of me but to take due care of them in their education?" He replied, "I know nothing about this. You know if God manifests to you that He requires something of you, there is nothing in the world which ought to hinder you from doing His will. *One must leave one's children to do this.*"

The War Cry, No. 145.—SEPT. 27, 1882.

A HEART TALK.

BY M. L. H.

OH, Lord, I am thine, save me. Thou hast redeemed me. Thy mercy has followed me. Thou hast not at all forsaken or forgotten me. All my days are filled with Thy goodness. There is no want to them that trust in Thee. They are filled because Thou art full, and they are united to Thee. I will praise Thee. Help me to praise Thee. Teach me, turn Thy face to me. Search me and try me. Refine the silver, weigh me in the balances. Be not afar off from Thy servant, oh, Lord, my Saviour, and my God.

Jesus, I love Thee, Thou art all love. Thou knowest if I *love Thee supremely*. If I love all else in Thee. Show me my own heart. Yea, Lord, earth's precious ones are Thine. I renounce them. They are Thine by my willing gift. Thou art Jesus, the first and the last. Thou art mine. Thou knowest if all my heart is Thine own. How shall I keep from Thee anything? Hast Thou not given me

Thyself, Thy Life, Thy death, Thy pains, Thy groans, Thy blood? Yea! Thou Prince of Saviours, Thou hast offered Thy sacrifice for me. I praise Thee, I love Thee first, Thou art my life, my light, my King, my joy, my crown. Thou art a jealous God; how shall I love Thee enough? Oh, Lord, let me abide in Thee! Here is rest, as of the weary babe in its mother's bosom. I lay me down in Thy arms. Love is my conqueror, I am His willing slave.

Master, I love and trust Thee. Increase my faith. May I not walk by faith? How faithful and worthy to be trusted is my God. How hateful is unbelief, how shameful. Oh, my soul hope in the Lord! Satan has designed to overthrow me. *Do I live in unshaken confidence always?* Thou knowest. He that doubteth is as a wave of the sea. I dare not doubt. My faith is small, but I dare not—I will not doubt Thee, my Lord and My God. Thou art in the darkness. Thou hast not forsaken me. Thou art nigh at hand. I shall praise Thee, for I do trust Thee. Father, Thou knowest all things. In sorrow I have leaned only on Thee. In loneliness Thou dost satisfy me. In afflictions I can trust Thee still. Yea, though Thou slay me, I am Thine altogether, to slay or to keep alive.

My faith looks up to thee; Thy sacrifice is my pardon, Thy blood my cleansing, Thy righteousness my Holiness. Keep me! Deliver me! Thou canst, Thou wilt, Thou dost. How strong Thou art, how good, how great. Hallelujah! Thou art my Salvation; my soul exulteth in God my Saviour; my faith takes hold on Thee. Thou art mine. Thou wilt guide me; thou wilt go before me. I will follow Thee all the way.

> "Faith knows nought of dark to-morrow,
> For my Saviour goes before."

My enemy is in Thy hands; Thou wilt smite him; Thou wilt answer his lying, doubting words. As for me, I trust in Thee, till I shall see Thee face to face.

Saviour may I serve Thee. I am not worthy to be called by Thy name. How can I fitly serve Thee? But Thou hast bid me. I praise Thee. I am Thy servant. What is Thy will? *A living sacrifice.* Oh, my Father, let Thy spirit search my life. What are my words, my deeds, my thoughts, my desires? Whence tend they? Thou dost ask a living sacrifice. Jesus, thou didst love the world. Thou didst die for it. Teach me so to love it, so to follow Thee. I am Thine. Make me a living sacrifice for Thy glory. Make me, mould me, break me. Thine is the altar, mine the offering. Accept Thy servant, a willing bond slave of love. Seal me Thine. Let me live to follow Thee. Thou art a seeker for the lost, a sufferer, a Saviour for the lost. Let me follow Thee. All I have shall serve thee. Write Thy name upon my heart, upon my forehead. Let me bear the Cross, and share the shame, and come after Thee. Let me be a good Soldier of Jesus Christ. All my life is given Thee. Every ransomed hour Thou hast. Blessed by Thy name. I am no longer my own. I am my Lord's, and He is mine. Glory to Jesus. The Cross shall wear the crown. All I have and all I hope belongs alone to the King of Glory. Hallelujah! Bless the Lord. Shiloh is come.

And Thou wilt accept Thy servant's offering. The love, and trust, and service of the humble is precious to Thee. Thy portion is Thy people. Thou dwellest with the contrite ones. Remember Thy child. Let Thy face be toward Thy servant for good. For Jesus Thy Son's sake. Amen.

CPSIA information can be obtained
at www.ICGtesting.com
Printed in the USA
FFOW01n1114120217
32253FF